ramtha
intensive

soulmates

Sovereignty, Inc.
Eastsound, WA

RAMTHA INTENSIVE:
SOULMATES

Edited by Steven Lee Weinberg, Ph.D.,
Carol Wright, John Clancy, and Pavel Mikoloski

DISCLAIMER

This book is designed to provide information in regard to the subject matter covered. The purpose of this book is to educate and entertain. The author, editors, and publisher shall have neither liability nor responsibility to any person or entity with respect to any loss or damage caused, or alleged to be caused, directly or indirectly by the information contained in this book.

ISBN 0932201-58-X
Library of Congress Catalog Card Number: 87-61225

FOR MORE INFORMATION:

For information about other books and audio and video cassettes presenting Ramtha's teachings, please write to: Sovereignty Inc., P.O. Box 926, Eastsound, WA 98245.

FIFTH PRINTING / MAY 1992
Book and Cover Design: Carol Wright

Sovereignty, Inc.

P.O. Box 926, Eastsound, WA 98245

Contents

RAMTHA INTENSIVE SERIES

Speaking through the body of JZ Knight, Ramtha has held more than 300 public audiences since 1978 in an effort to help awaken "gods asleep in the dream called mankind." Audiences presented prior to 1985 were called Dialogues because of their question-and-answer format. In early 1985, Ramtha began holding Intensives for the purpose of presenting more advanced teachings.

In 1986, Sovereignty published *RAMTHA,* the critically acclaimed best seller which presents the cornerstones of Ramtha's teachings as well as the fascinating story of Ramtha's lifetime. Sovereignty's Ramtha Intensive Series extends and complements the material presented in *RAMTHA.* Each volume in the Series presents an edited transcript of a select Intensive, supplemented with related material drawn from Sovereignty's library of Ramtha's teachings. Although it is not necessary to read *RAMTHA* prior to reading the volumes in the Intensive Series, the reader is encouraged to do so for a fuller appreciation and understanding of the material presented in the Series.

soulmates

*Here you are
learning to be God
in a grand intensive
that is enabling the
mate of your being
to perceive the beauty
of unlimited life.*

*Here you will learn
to wake up—together.*

Friday Morning Session
January 10, 1986

Ramtha, seated on the stage, observes the attendees as they file into the room and take their seats. He is dressed in a white sports outfit, the top of which is laced with rhinestones. After all attendees have settled in their seats, Ramtha picks up his glass of lemon water, rises from his chair, and walks forward.

Ramtha: (Raises his glass) To the bitter water. 'Tis the beginning of the dissolution of limited thought, that which does not *allow* knowledge to come forth. It is a cleanser of the body, and it represents the cleansing of the spirit. *(Raises his glass higher and toasts)* To Life!

Audience: To Life!

Ramtha: (After emptying his glass and placing it on the end table) You're going to drink a *lot* of it in this wondrous audience. So be it!

I am the *outrageous* Ramtha, and I am pleased to have you here this day in your time in this wondrous gathering.

(Models JZ's outfit, to the audience's delight) Contemporary, eh? It is called glitter, and I . . . glitter! Well, it is to change, perhaps, your notion of what angels are supposed to look like.

(After surveying the audience) This is a wondrous gathering. We have here that which is termed a collage, a mixture of entities who are here for different reasons. There are those of you who have come here to find your *soul*mates. Uh-huh. Then there are those of you who are here because you're, uh,

I am the outrageous Ramtha!

4

curious. Uh-huh! Then there are those of you here who want a lot, but you don't want to give much in order to get it. And there are many of you who were here at the last Soulmates Intensive. Didn't get enough? Need more runners, eh?

Well, *this* intensive on soulmates *is* a different session because it is a different time, it is a different "now" for the documentation of great knowledge. Unfortunately, there are not many of you who will take this knowledge and live it so that it becomes your future. But if I talk a lot and make a lot of things happen, sooner or later you will break down your barriers of ignorance. Then this grand knowledge can become the living consciousness of your nows.

So, you're a collage. You are that which makes up the human drama, the hu-man condition on this plane. But what each of you truly are is a grand god, a *grand* god. Most of you don't know that so well, but eventually, through experience, you are going to understand the meaning of "divine presence," the meaning of "God I Am," and the definition of the life of a christ.

All of you are indeed evolving, but *slo-w-w-w,* because you hold on to your belief systems. Know you what belief systems are? You hold on to your illnesses, your fears, your insecurities. You hold on to your dogmas, your ideals, your judgments. You hold on to them! Why? Because they give you your identity. If you didn't have your belief system you think you would not know what you are. Well, these teachings, given e'er so long ago in your time, are endeavoring, through wondrous ways, to break down the barriers of your belief systems so that you allow a movement of power to awaken within you. These words really won't mean anything to you until that power awakens. Only when you let go of your beliefs and peel away the layers of your limited self, will you come into a state of grace in which this knowledge will have absolute meaning.

Only when you let go of your beliefs will this knowledge have absolute meaning.

Every moment you are in this audience I am peeling away your limited beliefs to remove, little by little, your limited identities. As long as you are strapped with your limitations you're really a hearty burden to bear! Know you what burdens are? *(Jokingly)* Well, you are an intolerable mass! But the more you learn about you, the greater the light you will be to this plane, and the sooner you will see Superconsciousness—an end to the dilemma of the human drama, an end to all things that have plagued limitations upon your unlimited selves for e'er so long.

Now, soulmates! You are here to learn about this wondrous enigma. I'm going to begin by telling you that "soulmates" is a spiritual science. Know you the term "spiritual"? You think it means something unseen, don't you? Well, what do you call that which is *seen?*

Everything is spiritual. Because everything, even gross matter, is *volatile;* it is moving and changing.

Why do I call the understanding of soulmates a *spiritual* science? Because the understanding of soulmates transcends time, distance and space, the things that measure scientific understandings. So, *scientifically,* in its limited knowledge, there is no way to *prove* that you have a soulmate. So if you apply Galileo's theory to it, it won't work. If you apply Einstein's theory to it, it won't work. You get it? What I'm telling you is, you are *not* in a physics class!

Soulmates is a *spiritual* science. It is an understanding that goes *beyond* words, which puts us into quite a paradox. How can one teach about an unseen, spiritual science using practical words? He can't! There are no words. Because if words could describe it, it would be limited knowledge, and limited knowledge does not promote *un*limited understanding. It is a paradox that gives rise to the human drama.

So, how do I teach you about this great knowledge utilizing words? Well, I utilize words in long, lengthy processions—and in repetition—to spark an opening within you that allows the unspeakable knowledge to come through. Know you what the unspeakable truth is? The spiritual communication is *emotion.* Emotion! Emotion is Life itself, unspoken, quiet, profound movement.

Emotion is Life itself, unspoken, quiet, profound movement.

For many of you this is your first audience with that which I am. I will speak to you in a moment. But there are a few of

6

*I have changed
my speech because
I found
that few understood
"Indeed, so-be-it,
as-it-were-indeed,
as-it-is-now-seen."*

you here who have attended *many* of these audiences, who have been coming back for, perhaps, years. You think you've been studying a long time? When you sit on a rock and contemplate for seven years, *that* is a long time.

A point I wish to make about those who keep coming back to my audiences, is that I have been teaching them the same truths, over and over. Oh, I have changed my speech because I found that few understood "Indeed, so-be-it, as-it-were-indeed, as-it-is-now-seen." And when I would say, "What say you, beloved entity, who has come unto this plane, as it were indeed, to spin forth a drama, as it were, separate from the kingdom from which you came?" I lost them even before I got into the second part of the sentence! *(Throws back his head and laughs uproariously)* That's why when everyone wanted to quote me, they simply said, "Indeed." Well, that sort of says it all.

So it became very apparent that slang— Know you what slang is? Words like "okay," "oh, gosh," and others, which I shan't go into, but you know those words *very* well.

Entities would say to me, "A-w-w-right!" When I asked them, "What be 'awright'? What does that mean to you?" they would say, "It means 'okay.'" So I would ask them, "What means 'okay' unto you?" and they would reply, "Swell!" "What be a 'swell'? Is it liken unto an ocean?" "No. It is liken unto 'jazzy.' It's jazzy! That's what it is!"

So after many different words, I finally got down to the meaning. Because when they ran out of words, all that was left for me to see was their *emotion*. Then I knew what they meant! But in the process, I learned to speak your lingo, and I'm rather good at it.

So with new words, I kept telling the same thing to those who returned. Know you why? Because they weren't getting the simple message. They were *hearing* it, but they weren't *becoming* it. So I continued to manifest for them. I sent them here and there, and I made wondrous things happen in their lives. Yet all they wanted was *more*—not more of what *they* could do, but of what *I* could do for them! And it was *all* given, in love. But I still could not bring them to the understanding that they are God. I could not get them beyond that mountain because to them, it meant that if they *were* God, they had lost their identity. But know you what their identity is? One who is shrouded in limitation.

They could not get beyond that mountain because it just didn't sound right to put "God" on their license plate or driver's license. Why, they would be laughed right out of their homestead! But you see, thinking you must *say* you are God is also a limitation. You do not have to say it or wear it like an emblem! You only have to *be* it. Be it! Be!

I couldn't get them over the mountain. They wanted to hear something different. And yet, when you are God, you are *everything* different because you have unlimited genius—because you have the ability to *know,* which *is* everything. Why want all of the gold in the world when it is far greater to possess the knowingness that made it *and* the world of which it is a part? Is that not greater? Of course!

All that I was telling them was *this* close *(holding up thumb and forefinger)* to an understanding, but I could not bring them to that. Opening entities' eyes to their limited beliefs and having them give them up is an arduous battle, indeed.

Opening entities' eyes to their limited beliefs and having them give them up is an arduous battle.

Why do I teach about God, a subject that no one really cares about? *(Jokingly imitates audience)* "Let's get on with hopping in the sack with my soulmate!" *(Audience laughs.)* You see, your thoughts and your fantasies are *all* known. You may dress up and look prim and proper, but I see how you think.

Well, in the spiritual science of soulmates, there *is* great knowledge awaiting those who are ready to go on, who are ready to wake up from the dream they have been dreaming.

I delivered the first teaching on the science of soulmates to a sort of bewildered audience. They all came, hurry-scurry, thinking that the entity they might sit next to would be "The One." Know you "The One"? That is a part of your dream world. And I was hard-pressed in that audience to deliver a knowledge that is arduous to comprehend for those who have closed minds and are expecting a relationship. Because how

8

How do you teach knowledge to those with a closed mind?

do you teach knowledge to those with a closed mind, those who can't get beyond the mountain? If not through proper words, how do you deliver it?

I have contemplated that audience since then, and I have come up with some *spectacular* manifestations. You're gonna get it! *(Audience laughs.)*

Now, there are those of you who, even with this knowledge and the runners, are still going to be reticent to go over the mountain because you don't really want to get up off your rumps and *be*. Be! You are wanting to take this knowledge and put it away as a philosophy. Well, that is your option.

For three days I will teach you a grand, mystical truth that no one on your plane has ever defined. Oh, there have been speculations, but no one has ever *known* what the word "soulmate" meant. There have been speculations but never a true science of the word.

Science is knowledge. Enlightenment means "to be in knowledge of," for knowledge is the grandest treasure one can possess. It is not a treasure to possess God and the christ within you. You already *are* that! To possess knowledge so that you can *do* something with it is the wonderful thing.

Now I'm going to teach you the science of soulmates, but I'm going to talk around the subject, because the science is ethereal, it is beyond words. And I will teach you this knowledge only in segments, because I know where you are when I look at you; I see what you are absorbing and what you are not absorbing. I will teach only as long as the whole of this audience is absorbing.

Know you what "nature in the body" is? *(Looks at blank faces)* Ah! It is not a *mystical* term. It means you have to go to the bathroom. It means you are hungry, you have parched lips. When this audience has learned all it can and the energy is cohesive, at the peak, I will cease the teaching. Because if the body becomes uncomfortable, what you have learned will be dragged down by hunger and explosive kidneys. The body is a divine thing; it is part of, and the carriage for, a great god. It has to be attended to. *(Picks up his glass of water and toasts with the audience)* To Life!

Audience: To Life!

Ramtha: Now, for many of you, this intensive, as it is called, is going to last a *very* long time. Because the knowledge that I will give you, I will manifest for you until you get it—even if it takes the rest of your lifetime on this plane.

I have been asked to deliver within three days a knowingness that is not within time, that is not within dimensional understanding. It is not an understanding that you can measure to see if it is a biggie or a little. I will cover only parts of it to bring up a power that is needed for you to receive the emotions. I may deliver unto you a definition, an application, only for a short while. When the cohesive energy of this audience is at the peak of opening, you are going to be sent out and allowed to be with that emotional understanding for a moment. Do you understand? What I'm telling you is, I don't go by your watches!

Now, runners. They are very important in this audience. Know you what a runner is? They aren't entities who compete in races; they are manifestations. They are entities, thoughts, visions, experiences, and I will send you a lot of them. Why are you deserving this wondrous experience? Because the knowledge you are about to learn is learned only through experience. And what is experience? It is an *emotional* engagement, the feeling coming alive. Only through specific emotional engagements will you truly understand what I will endeavor to teach you with words.

Now, the runners are also called "miracles of knowledge." They are not coincidental. And no matter how much you try to reason them away, they shan't go away. I will send them to you so that what I teach you will be experienced in life, the wild adventure where "god discovers God." So be it!

Audience: So be it.

Ramtha: Now, know you that you are all dreamers asleep in a dream? A dreamer is one who lives in social consciousness, who is categorized in social consciousness, and lives by its modus operandi—you know, when you do only "nice" things

What I teach you will be experienced in life, the wild adventure where "god discovers God."

*It's not until
you wake up
from the dream
that you own
the wisdom of it.*

so as not to upset other entities, or want to "look good" so
that everyone will think you're quite marvelous. That is a
dream! And it's not until you wake up from the dream that you
own the wisdom of it. One of the great runners that will come
is a vision of being awakened from the dream.

What you will learn in this audience will wake you up to a
feeling, a knowingness, a cohesiveness, a singular self . . . understood, finally. And the runners? They will start to come,
straightaway. There will be a *host* of them, and they shall be
as unique as each of you are.

For three days you are going to sit here and you are going to
drink a *lot* of bitter water; it is wondrous for your body. And
you're going to learn a lot from what is *not* said because you
are going to *feel*. And you will sit in your little territories,
called your chairs, or your spot on this carpet that isn't Persian, and you're going to absorb. I'm not going to make you
"Om" or meditate or burn incense. I will simply give unto
you *knowledge,* for it is only knowledge that allows you to
transcend time and go into greater dimensions of life; to understand and embrace God, which is all things; and to live as a
light to mankind—as one who is without the appendages and
leeches that all of you carry upon yourselves.

All of you have adorned yourselves to come to this
audience. I am pleased. But do you know what I see when I
look at you? Imagine one who has wandered into the wilder-
ness, has fallen into a forsaken and wretched swamp, and he
has become *covered* with leeches! Know you what a leech is?
If you don't, I'll send you one so you'll have a practical dem-
onstration of their exact modus operandi. Well, when I look at
you, it's as if you are covered with layers that are liken unto
leeches. And the leeches are "not allowing." They are your
limited beliefs that do not *allow* your light to shine forth.

Many of you are shrouded in layers around your bodies. It
is seen in the unseen. What it is, is "limited mind," because
whatever you think and feel, manifests. If you know you are
wretched, so you are! If you know you're unhappy, so you
are! If you know you're unloved, so you are! Those are all

layers of limited beliefs that need peeling. And you have many layers on top of those, and the light of your auric field, the christ, is hidden like the sun behind clouds. *That* is what I see when I look at you. Understand?

Audience: Yes.

Ramtha: The runners are now at hand. One of their great duties is to help peel away all that keeps you in limitation so that you can begin to know. When you re-listen to my words, even a fortnight from now, what you heard this day will feel differently when you hear it again because the peeling away of your limited identities will have already begun.

You may not get everything I'm telling you for a long time. But when you do, time will stop for you. You will cease aging, and you will never be diseased again. And lo, you will have vision that will penetrate and go beyond the three-dimensional plane. It will take a long time or a short time, depending upon how quickly you peel and allow the light to come forward. You understand?

Audience: Yes.

Ramtha: So *be* it!

Now, know you of this entity, Ramtha, eh? Well, it is I. And I have come forth into the embodiment of my daughter. Why this wondrous guise? Because for ages, grand teachers have come to you and you have destroyed them all. You have muted their words; you have changed them. You are a fickle lot! Well, it shan't happen with *these* words. And here, I give you no image to gaze at, paint in long brush strokes, hang upon your wall, or wear around your necks. How tacky! There is no graven image of me anywhere that you can sit before and worship, for I shall not allow you to give your power away to me. And if you start to do this, I shall send you from this audience, straightaway. Do you understand?

Audience: Yes.

Ramtha: I am here to teach you that you are God so that you realize that the one you should have been loving, worshiping and adoring is *you* (you sort of missed the boat on this one for a long time); and so that, when you leave this audience, all

I shall not allow you to give your power away to me. If you start to do this, I shall send you from this audience, straightaway.

*That is going to be
a biggie
in these teachings:
love of self.*

you are left with are feelings, and new insights, and a new *love of self.* That is going to be a biggie in these teachings: love of self.

There is nothing in the seen or unseen that is greater than you. There never *has* been. Oh, you have dreamed them to be such, and you have given your power away to them; you have become subservient to them. No wonder you can't manifest anything! You don't have enough power left to pluck a fly off your nose! That is because you have given it away for *eons.* Give, give, give! Worship, worship, worship! Bow down and follow! You're very good at following, but you don't know how to lead. And leading does not mean gathering little groupies together and marching them off to some place. It means leading your *self: self*-vision.

It is the time for you to know yourself and to find God and the christ that are latent within you. The kingdom of heaven *is* within your vision because it is within feeling. The only way your plane will ever change (and it is going to) is when each entity realizes this.

There has never been anything created that is greater or less than you. There *are* entities in the unseen, a virtual host of them. But because they're unseen does not mean they're more powerful or more knowledgeable than you are. They are simply gods expressing in another frequency, another vibration, another plane.

Now, there are times you will curse me. That is all right; I will still be the wind, and I will still love you, in spite of your curses, because I do not *care* what you think of me. Nor do I care what your reporters think I am. I am a grand master, and that which I am, I *am,* forever and ever and ever. So what you think of me with your limited minds does not matter. What *you* think of *you* does! It does not matter where I came from, what I look like, or what I said thirty-five thousand years ago. Seeing who you are in the adventure called Self is all that is important. If you learn only the grand knowledge that you came here for, and we begin to peel from you your ignorance and limited beliefs, it really doesn't matter what I am, does it?

If my costume brings a few jolly laughs, that is all right also. One day you will know and see who be I, because that is when you will know and see yourself. Understand?

Audience: Yes.

Ramtha: Now, I have never been above—or below—doing *anything* to drive home a point. *(Audience laughs.)* Well, it is a truth! There are those who have lost fortunes, just to bring them to an understanding. There are those who have gained *everything,* just to prove that they could do it. It doesn't matter! I will do whatever is necessary. And my runners are such a motley lot that when the command is given they go and do their bidding. They will bring you a sequential understanding through which you will come to love what you are, deeply. And there will be moments when you are wholly alone, and yet you will find that that is *wonderful.* Whatever it takes to get the feeling across, the knowledge across, it will come.

Now, soulmates. "Well, finally he's getting on with it!" *(Audience laughs.)* Well, you see, it's always very smart to set the ground rules before you delve right into it.

Do all of you possess that enigma, that lover who comes in and out of your dreams, that immaculate vision of knighthood or womanhood? Indeed! All of you do! There is not *one* entity who does not possess a soulmate.

You know, a wondrous thing about mankind: once you tell him something *belongs* to him, there are only a few things he won't do to get it—even though he doesn't *understand* what he is wanting! He wants it only because someone says it belongs to him. Well, that can be very advantageous to learning.

All of you have a soulmate. For ten million years you have had one. Do you need one? Oh, absolutely! *(Raises his glass for a toast)* To soulmates!

Audience: To soulmates.

Ramtha: Now, your first runner. I am sending the lot of you a manifestation of the image of what you think the perfect man or perfect woman is. I want you to get caught up in your fantasies. Know you what a fantasy is? Of course you do! You are going to get caught up in your fantasy of your perfect lover.

All of you have a soulmate. For ten million years you have had one.

So be it! *First* runner.

Now, a soulmate isn't a thing; it isn't an object! It is a soul/spirit entity that is, or had been, a humanoid. Know you that you are all humanoids? Not a very pretty word, "humanoids." But that's what you are after all: God manifested into fleshy stuff.

There are very few entities who ever find their soulmates, ever! All of you have lived *lifetimes* without ever seeing the other part of yourselves. Why haven't you gotten together? Why haven't you met that person? Well, there are those of you who *thought* you had met your soulmates, but that lasted only for a little while and then sort of ran out of steam. So you realized that that wasn't the entity—because certainly your soulmate would be sustaining and fulfilling and *everything* you desire. Well, you're asking an awful lot of someone else, aren't you? What about *you?* Are *you* desirable? Are *you* fulfilling? Are *you* a joy to be around? Are you inspiring? Are you humble? Do you possess honor, integrity, virtue? *Do you?* In other words, if I say, "Behold! Look at the door! Come forth, soulmate!" and you turn around to see, with great anticipation, what your soulmate looks like, what would you do if it was *you* walking in the door, with all of *your* hangups and limitations?

It is undivinely selfish to expect someone else to make you happy. You don't deserve it. Know why? Because if you haven't loved yourself enough to make yourself happy, *who* wants to pick up the broom and "go to it"? No one *I* know of.

Now, second runner. I am sending you a dream. In the dream will come a lover (or you will think that the entity is). You will be waiting with outstretched arms, and there will come an entity wearing a mask. Know you what masqueraders are? The entity will be everything you thought a soulmate *shouldn't* be. And you will tell yourself to wake up and get out of this stupid dream, but the entity wearing the mask will just *drag* you down. And you will go through such a dream that you will think it has lasted a hundred years! At the end of the dream, when morning is on the horizon and golden rods are piercing through the veil of night, you'll wake up from your slumber—but not before you got aggravated enough to take the mask off of the entity, only to see that it was *you*. In other words, you're gonna get a bedfellow for a night, and it will be you. Understand?

Audience: Yes.

Ramtha: Now, I desire for this to be a *very heavy* dream. And you are going to remember it all. For only when you know *you* can you start cleaning up your act. Bargain?

Audience: Bargain.

Ramtha: So be it.

What makes *you* such a terrific gift to someone else? You're not very terrific, for you are one who can neither give nor receive, because you are hung up with so many illusions. So I will send the runners, and we will do what is called a housecleaning. When you are not honorable I will send back your *dis*honor one hundredfold! When you are not compassionate, when you do not feel and cannot forgive because your altered ego will not allow you to be humble, I will send to you a tormenter who is ruthless, one hundredfold! When you are not merciful, merciful!— Know you what it is to have mercy? What do you do when you meet someone who is "down and out," as you term it? How much money does it take to make you *un*merciful?

I have seen you be merciful with animals. I have seen your tenderness with insects. (There are still a few insects that really haven't brought up mercy inside you, but eventually you will be able to talk to them and tell them to be on their way.) But when it comes to *gold* you are a ruthless lot. Ruthless! I have sent tests to some of you and I have seen you be unmerciful for the sake of a dollar! I am going to send it back to you, one thousandfold, until you learn that the virtue of mercy has no price. No matter how much someone owes you, is it worth bringing yourself down by being ruthless, unforgiving, unallowing?

You know, you're *very* petty. You want to be enlightened, but you're very petty. What is gold worth? What is getting

How much money does it take to make you unmerciful?

even worth? What are those things worth compared to the timeless flow called life forever? Can you take them with you? No! But you *will* take with you the unmerciful feeling, because that remains in the soul. And that is a leech, a layer that lines your body and covers the light.

I am going to cause a little bit of havoc in your life. There are entities who owe you yen, marks, rupees, shekels, dollars, pence—whatever you call gold. And up till now they've been very good about repaying. But all of a sudden they're not going to give it to you any longer because they have problems. I want to see how much weight you put on their shoulders so that you can live frillfully. So we're going to call a little halt to it. I want to see how unlimited, how merciful, how virtuous you can be. I will send you three of those runners. So be it!

Now, do you know what "groupies" are? They're like herd animals. They stick together. And they like to gang up on others. They gossip about the other animals. They can never get along amongst themselves, but they have to stay together.

Well, I have seen you gang up on others. I have seen you create a truth, called gossip. I have seen you, through that truth, take away the beauty and the joy of another. I am sending back your condemnations, one hundredfold, so that you experience what you have placed upon another.

Do you know what honor, integrity and nobility are? No, you don't! Because *those* are not a part of your identity. Know you how to live in grace? No, but you're *going* to know. I am sending runners to you to teach you how to be honorable, how to be forgiving, and how to love. What do these have to do with the reason you came to this audience? It is a part of cleaning you up to make you presentable to your soulmate—because *your* ideal possesses *all* of these virtues.

Do you have to have your soulmate in order to become God? You will always have that entity/essence with you, but no, you do not. Do you have to live with your soulmate in order to be happy? No. Do you need to go out and find your soulmate? No. The knowledge that I will teach you these days and the runners that will come will give you the understanding of why I answer this way.

Now, I am going to take you back to the beginning of creation so that you understand what the science of soulmates means. It would take a lifetime to explain the process, so I will give you only a very short synopsis of the eternal mystery of how it all began. You will get the picture. If you don't I'll send you a vision so you can see it.

Now, God. You think of God in many different ways. Your reality conceives of the all-wise knowing intelligence in many forms. But in a greater understanding, God is Thought. Before there was a beginning, there was only Thought—without light, without movement, without matter.

If I removed every star, every planet, every sun from this universe (in other words, took a vacuum cleaner and vacuumed it up), what would you see? You wouldn't see anything because there wouldn't be any light. You could only perceive. (Now, this is heavy stuff!) Without light, the eye cannot see; it cannot perceive movement.

Thought, which is God, does not move; it *is*. What allows movement is Light. Without Light, there is only empty space, without dimension, without measure, with no beginning and no end . . . the forever Now.

What do you think holds up your world? What keeps you from falling off it? What is it? You say it is empty space! No, it is Thought, the Is. That is the platform called forever.

There came an hour when Thought turned inward and contemplated its vastness. In other words, Thought thought about itself. When it did that, Light was born. That was the birth of Knowledge.

Light, as you know it, is made up of particum. In particum, you have the positive/negative electrum that keeps it cohesive and explosive. But in its highest form, light is undivided particums that contain and hold all of its potential lower units. And each light particum is a cohesiveness of individual, expressive thought.

You were born of God, of Is, of Space, if you will, when Thought contemplated itself and the contemplation became

When Thought turned inward and contemplated its vastness, that was the birth of Knowledge.

Light, the Movement. So, in your beginning each of you became a particum of light. That is your highest, *individual* form. So, all of you prevailed in the beginning. You *were* "the beginning," because *you* created time.

Know you how electricity was created? By lowering light. Because if you take light and lower it (meaning: slow its frequency), you divide it into a positive/negative fuse; thus you get magnetic fields. Did you know that? *(Seeing blank expressions in the audience)* You *don't* know that. Well, maybe this *will* be a physics class! But the only way you get a magnetic field is by having a negative and a positive energy.

When the Is contemplated itself and gave birth to Movement, birth to Light, that was when all of the gods were born. Each of you became a light particum, a whole, a god. And the gods, immediately endowed with souls, created from their thought processes.

From the light particums were created the gases that created what your scientists think was a "big boom," a large blast—you know, when boom! everything sort of happened. Well, you can say that, if you want to try to measure time, but it didn't quite happen that way. That is only measuring time. You have to forget about time in order to know. But it was the gods who created everything thereafter through the souls of their beings.

Now, I know where many of you *think* the soul is. But it isn't in your head. Your soul sits here, in a cavity next to your forever muscle, your heart. In the cavity, there is a light essence, and it weighs thirteen ounces. When you are feeling love in your soul, you think it is coming from your heart. But your heart is only a pump; it doesn't get in love with anything. It's the soul that feels.

The only way that the light particums, or the gods, could create from the thought coming from their Father, the flow of thought that gave them life, was to have something, which is termed the soul, which could hold the thought still. I call the soul the lord of your being. The *god* of your being is your spirit. It is the grand light that envelops the whole of what you are. Understand?

Your soul is like a computer. It holds and stores thought. Without your soul you would know no thing, you could express no thing, you could create no thing, you would *be* no thing, except Is. The soul records every thought you've ever had. It does not record it as a thought, but rather as what the thought electrically did to your light form; it's called feelings. Feelings are the basis of the gaseous matter of your universe; they *created* gaseous matter.

*Feelings
are the basis
of the gaseous matter
of your universe;
they created
gaseous matter.*

Heard you of atoms? That is another universe. What gives substance to the atoms, the inner universe, is a particle that is called the Z particle. That was the first feeling *manifested,* and it gave life to the whole of your universe.

Matter was born from the great suns. They lowered the electrum to create gaseous matter, particles of which scattered for endless time. And all along, space, the quiet, the void, called Thought, allowed light to play upon it. So, matter is born, but the gods, the light particums, still prevail.

Gods created the first livable planet in your solar system. It was called Melina, and it was the first planet birthed from your sun. It was created from light giving birth to mass, a natural process. There the gods played, creating light forms. (At this point, you, the gods, are each still one god, *undivided.* So, you are without gender, as it were.) When, through their competitive spirit, the gods destroyed Melina (remnants of it now circle Saturn), many of them went to the far reaches of your universe, where they still are this day in your time. Others went to the planet that is in line with your Earth but on the other side of the sun, a planet which your scientists will discover before the end of this century. So there is another planet out there that you didn't know you had.

After Melina was destroyed, your Earth, called Terra, evolved from the side of your mother sun and was set into orbit. Through its rotation it cooled. In time (we are talking of billions and billions of years, where there really is no time), it was impregnated and ready for life.

Have you ever seen the planet Venus? If you haven't I'll

send you a photograph of it. Did you know that this planet is the new Earth?

Venus is covered in clouds, is it not? Why do you think the clouds are there? They are oceans in the stratum, which will one day be the oceans on that planet. Life is coming to be on the surface of that planet through aqueous substance. It is a paradise there. The temperature is constant because the cloud cover is a conduit for light. It takes the light from the sun and disperses it evenly around that planet. Thus the whole of that planet is like a warm womb in which new life-forms are developing, just like it happened here. It is a reaction and another play, another drama happening. *(Picks up his glass and proposes a toast)* To creation! May you know it all!

Audience: To creation!

Ramtha: So your Earth evolved. A cloud cover once surrounded it, just like one now surrounds Venus. Your vast oceans used to be this cloud cover. In time, life here came to a three-dimensional, aqueous substance level. So now we have come from light to water. And the gods, through their desire, through their souls, created the cellular mass of every life-form upon your Earth.

The gods, through their desire, through their souls, created every life-form upon your Earth.

Think about this for a moment: Have you ever watched an exotic hummingbird gathering nectar from a lily? If you haven't, I'll send you one. So be it! Have you ever watched the metamorphosis of a worm into a splendidly-arrayed butterfly? If you haven't, I'll send you one. Have you ever seen the pearl hue of a fish in a babbling brook at midday? Have you ever seen a rainbow underneath the sea? If you haven't, I'll send you to where you can see one.

Have you ever counted how many species of insects there are? Have you ever counted the species of the animal kingdom? Have you ever held up a crystal and looked through it at a noon sun, an evening sun, or by the light of the moon? And how many kinds of flowers are there? How many species of ferns are there? And who decided that moss would always grow on the north side of things to be a lantern unto a passerby? Who created those things?

Who taught the great heron how to fish in the sea by scaring the fish and running them into shore, and then shade his eyes with his wing while he looks into the water to see them? *Who* gave him that intelligence? Who gave the intelligence to a flower so that it would smell like rotting meat, even *look* like rotting flesh? Who designed it so it would attract a fly to go in and lay its eggs inside the flower to create maggots, which would be digested by the flower? *Who* created that? Who created the grand plant to grow a leaf so broad that it would wrap around itself to collect the morning dew, drop by precious drop, so that a very special little frog could live there and keep it company? Who created that? Who gave it that sublime knowledge?

Which one of you Egyptians from a past life created the Egyptian stork that could pick up a stone so that he could break the egg of an ostrich by dropping the stone on it until it cracked? Which one of you clever entities taught him that?

Who taught the salmon how to live and frolic in a far, far sea? And when their lives were spent and their souls were heavy with experience, who taught them how to bring forth a new generation so that they themselves could come back as their own young and feed off the rotting flesh of their former bodies, now lying still in a pure stream? Who taught them how to do that? Hmm?

Which one of you women taught a gazelle how to run like a little dancer, seemingly born of wings? Who taught her how to give birth to her babe? Who whispered in the babe's ear to stay still like a stone? And who gave the babe the knowingness to emit no smell? Who did these things?

These are only a few of the wonders of this life, but know you who did all of these things? *You* did. Know you *how* you did it? By feeling from the Is and captivating that emotion within your souls. You felt everything into life. You breathed life into those creative, aqueous forms, called cells. You gave the cells a *pattern*.

Did you know that each cell possesses the pattern of the whole? Did you know that from a scraping of tissue from your

Which one of you women taught a gazelle how to run like a little dancer, seemingly born of wings? Who whispered in the babe's ear to stay still like a stone?

nose, your scientists can clone your double? It's true.

You breathed life into what you created by feeling it into existence. This "breath" was not that it could be a breathing creature. The breath of life was "patterns of destiny." You gave your creations their intelligence, which would go on and on and on. Sound absurd? Well, there is far more to the story. I will send you runners of vision, and they will fill in the blanks where no words come. So be it!

Audience: So be it.

Ramtha: Now, did you know that thought can pass through matter? Well, you have visions of spiritual entities and ghosts who pass through walls, right? They *do,* because they are vibrating at a higher frequency than the three-dimensional frequency. Three-dimension is mass, which is coagulated thought, but a thought can pass through it.

What did this mean to you? It meant that although you had breathed the patterns of destiny into your creations, into the whole of this world, you couldn't smell the rose you created or touch that furry little creature called an otter. You couldn't coddle, smell, taste, hear, see. You could only *perceive.* The only way you could be a part of this thriving kingdom was to lower your frequency and condense *yourself* into mass. And that is when you really got into trouble.

The only way you could be a part of this thriving kingdom was to lower yourself into mass. That is when you really got into trouble.

The gods created and possessed bodies so that they could experience the kingdom they created here. And I must tell you, if we brought forward one of those bodies this day, you would be horrified. Horrified! Because it wasn't what you would call beautiful. But it was a wondrous vehicle that allowed the gods to go in and out of this kingdom.

Now, in the beginning of the experiments with man, bodies were just made. You know bodies? Well, they're sort of like your wardrobe. You had a selection of them, but they were without gender. And it was very easy for a god to create a body. All he had to do was *think* it and *feel* it, and it became! That's how you manifest everything.

Now, there came an hour when the gods desired to create bodies that reflected the uniqueness of each god. So they contemplated, like the Is once did, and they came up with the idea of creating male *and* female bodies that could copulate to bring forth the species called human. The only problem was, no god wanted to become either male *or* female! So they conceived of becoming *both,* by lowering and splitting themselves. That meant lowering their light and their souls, lowering them from the pinnacle of light to the lower electrums where *division* occurs—because if you take this grand light and lower its frequency, it soon splits to become the polarity of positive/negative.

So the gods lowered their light. When it became positive/negative, the light and the soul split. And it would stay split as long as it was in a lower frequency.

Whew! Got through that one! Creation is always a toughie! *(Raises his glass in a toast)* To the split!

Audience: To the split.

Ramtha: So, gods created two bodies through cellular design, one to house the positive charge and one to house the negative charge. The negative would be called the female gender, the positive would be the called male gender. The hormones would flow in the body according to the electrical charge housed in it. The thing that would open the doors to the hormone flow would be the electrum energy in the body.

So, in the female the doors were set. When the female energy, the negative energy, possessed a body designed to house that energy, it turned the locks, all seven seals opened up, the flow of "hormone balance" began, and behold! the female was born. Into the male, who also had the seven doors, the seven seals, the seven chakras, the positive energy entered. The hormones began to flow, and behold! the masculine entity was born. Remember, we are talking of one god splitting and becoming one set of bodies: positive *and* negative.

The penis, the loins, the breast, the nest, the vagina—these did not exist in the cellular mass of the body at the moment of its creation. It was the hormones' control, their *harmony,* that would bring these things into being.

So, the negative charge entered the female body. As the

23

The only problem was, no god wanted to become either male or female! So they conceived of becoming both.

body was in slumber, the breasts grew, the body softened and took form, because the seven ductless glands were now open and secreting hormones—*harmony*. The soul-spirit split was in harmony with that body. The positive charge entered the ''clay'' of the male body, turned the locks of the seven doors, and the body began to grow into masculine form.

So awaken from slumber man! awaken from slumber woman!—soulmates, looking into one another's eyes, *seeing* self for the first time ever! seeing the reflection, the energy! feeling both of their souls and spirits sharing the same experience, except in a different version. Are you beginning to see? Are the lights turning on? *(Picks up his glass for another toast)* To Life!

Audience: To Life!

Ramtha: Now, hear you the term "genetics"? Contemplate for a moment the science of genetics. Think about what makes genetic memory.

Each of you possesses, in your loins and in your womb, seeds that contain the genetic memory to create another entity. What do you think is creating the chromosomes that carry genetic memory? Well, what created *everything?* Feelings! Genetic memory is created through *emotion*.

Ten million years ago, the gods split to become male/female energy; and every adventure they had in matter brought forth emotion.

Ten million years ago on your plane the gods split to become male/female energy; and every adventure they had in matter brought forth emotion. Every moment they felt something of high emotion, the chromosome structures inside the sperm and egg received an imprint. *That* is what is creating your body, right this moment. That is the science the gods devised to create new bodies with new characteristics that would be different rather than clones.

So, soulmates are ''born.'' They copulate. But before copulation, the man is running from a predator. As he runs he is desiring with great emotion for his legs to be longer and swifter. In that moment, he creates a new pattern on his chromosome structure, through *desire*. So, the chromosomes are changed. He runs back to his hovel to find his mate, who during the day had been joyful in spirit; so, in her chromosomes there is the imprint ''happy life.'' They copulate and a physical body is conceived, one which will have, genetically, happy cells and longer legs!

Other gods, now splitting, start choosing their bodies from the offspring of soulmates. The positive energy from the split chooses a body with a positive charge. When he comes in, it is a new adventure of smell and harmony, of suckling for the first time at his mother's breast, of being carried on his father's shoulder and getting a spectacular view of a meadow. And when he grows to full height he will have long limbs and he will outrun his father. And his father will say, ''You are, indeed, the son of my desire.'' You see how it works?

Audience: Yes.

Ramtha: What evolved you genetically? What caused evolution? What caused the ongoingness? What caused your skin to get finer and your head to get bigger? *Feelings*. Because every moment, your emotions are manifesting. And guess what is recording them all? The lord of your being, your immortal soul. So for ten million years you have lived on this plane and you have evolved through emotions.

Soulmates *shared* the paradise of life here, because each was receiving from the other the greatest gift of all, feelings. The joy of the woman birthing the child—that *feeling* was given to the mate of her being, the other part of herself, her soulmate. What wondrous ''psychic'' experience was going on here? They were the *same* soul, *same* spirit, and whatever one experienced the other felt.

The next lifetime, they made the choice, perhaps, to be in different lands from one another because those are the bodies they picked for their next adventure into life.

Where is *your* soulmate right now? There are those of you here whose soulmates are on this plane at this moment. There are others whose soulmates are on another plane at this moment, or in another universe at this moment. Know you what connects you together? Feelings. You are always this close. *This* close!

So the one god split and became two individuals, soulmates; yet it still remained whole, one god. Their thoughts, which manifest as feelings, flow between them. You are attached to your soulmate liken unto some divine elastic cord. It can stretch into forever and yet it always remains intact. You're as close to your soulmate as a breath away, a moment away, a passion away; because, remember: time, distance and space do not measure or separate the unseen, do not measure the Is, called Life.

I know what some of you are thinking. "I *know* my soulmate is in the Pleiades," for that gives you a sort of arrogance. Well, be done with that. "Well, maybe another place, perhaps some exotic foreign land." Do you think going there and finding them is going to be a wondrous experience? For most of you it won't, because you are steeped in prejudice. Aren't you? And you would have an arduous time accepting someone of another race, another color.

What about the young, muscular man who every day works out? He runs nowhere, he lifts dumbbells, and he gains muscular tone, rippling down his chest—and yet he fights no battles! How vain! And he dreams of his dream lover (except there's no room for her because he keeps looking in the mirror at himself). Well, his soulmate is eighty-one years old! Now, wouldn't that be a blow to his altered ego?

You see, many of you are lost in social consciousness—in beauty, prosperity, wealth, fame, power. Those are your hang-ups; that is your whole dream. You want to be beautiful, vo-*lump*-tu-ous. You want to be the most famous. And you want to be *powerful,* to have clout. You want these things because they somehow lift you above the ordinary and mundane. But you are living in a box! Well, I've got a lot of runners coming in regard to your box, and I'm going to close the walls in on you. Because if you are looking for *knowledge,* you must transcend the limited specter of social consciousness.

There are those of you who hold the dogmatic belief that you are part of a "soul family," that you have been together with other entities for lifetimes! But wouldn't it be sort of boring to be married to the *same* old husband or wife, have the *same* bratty kids for ten million years? Reason it. Use your brain, this receiver of yours, and reason it!

You see entities who are familiar to you. If you go to a psychic, they'll tell you exactly who they've been to you. And you'll accept it, even if it doesn't feel right. Well, those entities *are* familiar, but they could have been the husband, the wife, the sibling, the mother, the father of your *soulmate*. That is where the familiarity comes from, because the two of you *share* knowledge. The dummy lifting the bells and the old woman knitting with gnarled fingers are sharing that experience, and that pain, and that subtle grace with each other.

You and your soulmate experience, you learn, you *share*. What your soulmate has experienced, you have experienced, and vice versa, because you share knowingness, you share understanding with each other.

Know you the word "psychic"? Is that not a very seductive, mystical, contemporary term? Know you that everyone in this room *knows*. You don't need to ask anybody about your future, just take a look at what you're doing now and what you're thinking now.

Everyone here is a psychic. To prove this I am sending another runner to you. You are going to know something, and within three days, behold! it will come to pass. Then you can put "psychic" on your business card and the shingle on your auto-machine. (I wouldn't advise that, because when you start telling other people about their future, they'll hold you responsible for it.) I will send that manifestation so all of you get an inkling that you *do* know.

Where does some of your knowingness come from? How do you "psychically" know some things? Because more than likely, at that moment, your mate is experiencing it and you are receiving their feelings. That's how you know.

Why do you crave some things? Have you ever walked in the marketplace and, out of nowhere, comes a vision of a luscious peach hanging from a tree. You see nectar oozing out of it and you want it! So you go looking high and low for one until you find one. You bite into it, and oh! how sweet it is!

What your soulmate has experienced, you have experienced, and vice versa, because you share knowingness, you share understanding.

Where did that craving come from? Perhaps at that moment, your soulmate had just plucked the peach, rubbed it on its khaki shirt, took a nice, luscious bite out of it, and it drove you mad! That is where cravings often come from. If you are hungry for something it is often because your mate is having it for dinner. If you are having an urge to strip your clothes off and swim in a pond, it's because your soulmate has declothed and taken a wonderful swim in a pond somewhere, and it is so refreshing! That is where desires often come from, and they go back and forth. Everything you do, your soulmate is experiencing—but not with the physical body, with the spiritual body. Are you understanding?

Audience: Yes.

Ramtha: You and your soulmate are connected for all time. When we take a look at your past, we consider two entities, not one. The two of you are one god on an amazing journey. You are one god expressing as both man *and* woman. And whether or not you ever come together, you always represent that oneness, that wholeness, that is neither male nor female but both of them. And for ten million years the two of you have been experiencing this plane, together. What is that commercial? "Double your pleasure"?

You are at a point to think about this understanding for a wee bit. Go to the watering hole, go to the latrine, move your bodies around, and return here in only a few moments. We shall continue. So be it!

Audience: So be it.

The two of you are one god on an amazing journey. You are one god expressing as both man and woman.

***

Friday, Second Session
January 10, 1986

After the members of the audience have returned from the break and have settled in their seats, Ramtha begins his address for the second session.

Ramtha: All beloved masters who have heard this teaching before, rise to your feet and stay put for a moment. *(They stand.)* All of you in this section who have *not* heard this teaching before, arise and be seated where these entities are. I want all of you "old pros" in one section. So, do change. *(Everyone starts talking at once and moving around.)* There's nothing like a little confusion, eh?

Woman: Ramtha, do you mean the ones who have been to *any* intensive, or just the previous intensive on soulmates?

Ramtha: (Shouting) I am referring to all of those who had been to the last soulmates teaching. You, sit in this area. Those of you who haven't, take their places. I am having you exchange territories. Isn't it wonderful; you get to sit beside someone who you weren't sitting beside before.

(After everyone is settled) Now, this is where the teaching begins to divide a bit.

(Turns to the "old pros") So, you have been segregated from the lot. We are going to teach all, but your runners are going to be different than those who are new to this audience.

(Picks up his glass and toasts with the audience) To Life! Forever, and ever, and ever! So be it!

Audience: So be it!

This is where the teaching begins to divide a bit.

30

Ramtha: Now, I let you go to contemplate a little bit, and you contemplated just a little—and that's about it! You were wandering all around, "checking everyone out." Well, masters, if I were to check *you* out, you wouldn't be sitting here any longer.

In the introduction I gave you, we talked of the "slings and arrows" of creation and your having come to a dividing point, a parting of ways. So, you are now getting a sense of what a soulmate is. It's your *other* self.

Now, there is no such thing as your *higher* self or *lower* self. Did you know that? It does not behoove you to speak of your "higher self," because when you do, that always lowers you. Did you know that? For if part of you is higher, another part must *always* be lower.

Spiritual dogma is riddled with spirits and guides, seemingly powerful unseen entities who are thought to be grander, higher, and more powerful than you. Entities, there is nothing grander than *you,* nothing!

You don't possess a higher self. If you want to believe that you do, you are copping out on yourself. Did you know that? When you are endeavoring to "get it together"— Know you what "getting it together" really means? It's a wondrous term! It means coming from negative/positive into center, for that's where peace lies. Getting it together is much more difficult if you have "multudious" selves to try to corral and get it together with! You have to reach up and pull down your higher self and pick up your lower self.

If you want to believe that you have "multudious" selves, you are giving your power away to a dogma—a created truth without the substance of validity. You understand? You're *riddled* with dogmas! And they are one of the things that cover up your light.

God *is.* The Is is like the simplicity of a line. It is simple, simple, simple!

Know you what genius is? It is to captivate simplicity. Know you what intellect is? Complexity. Complexity is limitation; simplicity is unlimitedness. Do you understand?

*Know you
what genius is?
It is to captivate
simplicity.
Know you
what intellect is?
Complexity.*

With your intellect and your complexities, you make a big deal out of everything! You make so much of a simple thing that it is very hard for you to wake up from the illusion to see reality.

Now, endeavoring to impart knowledge to you about the science of soulmates is like working through a maze. And you created the maze with dogmas, limited beliefs and a closed mind. And the more you close down your mind, your wondrous receiver, the more limited you become and the greater the maze grows.

Every moment you *believe* in something, you give your power away to the belief. Did you know that? No wonder you are sick! No wonder you can't even heal yourself! You can't make anything happen because your only "food" for thought is what others think rather than the genius you have ready access to. You are living off what is called "social consciousness." You are living off the limited thoughts of others. You are living for a "groupie" effect. Whenever you do that you give away your power.

(To the newcomers) I have separated you from this lot. They are already receiving runners. They are already on their way. I am going to give them a boost. But they are still in a maze, just like you are.

Now, though I'm speaking to you individually, you *and* your soulmate are going to hear this message. Because what you feel in this audience, your mate will feel also. Your soulmate will get psychic flashes of this happening.

Now, union of self. Each of you has another "you." The other is not higher or lower; it is simply the other. In an unlimited form it is called "I Am." Did you know that "I Am" is the All-in-All, without walls, boundaries and appendages? Did you know that "I Am" is the declaration of the unity of self, forever and ever and ever? That describes you—and the other "you" that you are.

Now, hear me! You have a very nasty, *nasty* habit of not listening to everything I say. You like to pluck out phrases and say, "That is law!" You take part of the teachings, and that's

*I am going to send you
a fanatic.
The reason for this?
I want you to be aware
of how I feel
talking to you!*

what you hold on to. But what about the *other* things I said? If you wish to learn, then hear *everything,* not just what you *want* to hear. Listen to it all! If you don't, you will become a *fanatic!* Know you what they are? I am going to send you a fanatic, one who never got it all, only parts. They can be from any cult or religion, whatever. I am sending one to you, and you are going to pull your hair out! The reason for this? I want you to be aware of how *I* feel talking to *you.* So be it! And I am going to sit and have a jolly good laugh!

(To the "old pros") Now, back to you! You pluck from the *continuum* of this teaching only the things you are wanting to hold on to. And you sit there, patiently, waiting to hear it, nodding your heads and drinking your water, and you finally hear what you are wanting to hear. And boy! do you leap for joy! Because taken out of context the statement confirms a dogma that you own. Yet, when you do that you are a fanatic! And when you are fanatical, you are not coming from nega-tive/positive to center space; you are going to one extreme; you are tipping the scales.

There are many entities who say they love me greatly, yet they are always taking my teachings out of context—and they do it in *my* name. Know you the term "fed up." Know you what that means? I am not pleased.

When I teach you, I render a *complete* understanding, along with the miracles. Certainly you can pick out of it what you want to. But do not pick out of it and then say it represents the *whole* of my teaching, for it doesn't! You shan't *ever* under-stand the whole of this teaching until you are without limited form, because that's what *I* am!

Fanatics are dogmatic entities. They get caught up in partic-ular phrases, and those become their truth, their lord, their beacon, their fire, their flame. And they forget about being and allowing—those divine words that express an unlimited, moving joy that all of you have. You get caught up in words or little phrases and you throw away the joy, the love, the con-nection, the *super*-connection.

Fanatics soon become even more limited in their truth. And

so angry and frustrated and unhappy are they, that they soon set themselves above the rest of the world. They would even go to the depths of *slaying* the rest of the world to prove their point, their truth! *Woe unto you if you take what say I out of context and become fanatical with it,* for I will send to you that limited truth *one thousandfold,* until you say, "Enough! What *were* the other things he said?" Bargain?

Audience: Bargain.

Ramtha: So be it!

All I have ever said, and all the words I have ever formulated and issued forth, have all been for one great understanding: *You are God.* Because, when you realize this, then you are *everything.* Then there are no wars, there are no beliefs, there are no illusions. There is only life—splendid, unlimited. When you fully realize this, you have regained your power, wholly! And that power is what has opened up your receiver, such that if your arm were ever severed from its socket, you could say, "Come forth!" and another one would grow in its place in a moment. It is a power such that all you have to do is desire to see the other side of the sun, and you would be there in a moment. It's *that* kind of power! And not *one* of you has reclaimed it.

All I have ever said is that you are God. And when that is known, joy is the prize and life is the epic adventure where that can be displayed.

Soulmates are God. They are God! You and your soulmate are not *one-half* God, with a fractional interest in the other half! You are, wholly, individually, right where you are, born/lived, a god. The grand adventure of the two of you is to embark upon life, wake up from the dream, be enriched with the knowledge of the dream, and go from limited mind into unlimited mind. What do you think Superconsciousness is? It is Unlimited Mind. It is when all of your brain is operational.

Soulmates are God. You and your soulmate are not one-half God, with a fractional interest in the other half!

You think you're so intelligent? Did you know that you are using less than one-third of your brain power? So, tell me you are smart.

There are those of you who are in a process of an inward

34

collapse, and your brain is shutting down, because you are *decadent* entities. You have lost the moral virtue of the joy of life. And when your brain shuts down, you are no more on this plane. No more.

To learn what I am teaching you is to feel it, *all* of it! Not to repeat phrases! That teaches you nothing!

For eons you've had a nasty habit of taking things out of context. You have altered and re-written the message of every grand teacher who has ever been on this plane because you wanted to see their truth differently. Thus you have changed the values of knowledge. Well, this shan't happen with this that I teach you, for it is to remain pure, forever and ever, for your sake.

Not one of you here, or anyone who has ever attended these audiences, can speak on my behalf. You can only speak on your own. These teachings are to remain pure so that they have the stability to remind you that you are a light in the world. When you have experienced your runners and your life has changed, and, perhaps, you've forgotten what was at the end of the rainbow, you can come back and listen anew, for these teachings will still be there. It is called forever. And it will keep you focused on center so that you can go on. You understand?

Audience: Yes.

Ramtha: Now, the search for soulmates. There are those of you who are willing to throw away your husbands, your wives, your lovers, to go in search of the unicorn. You are willing to abandon your families and give up your meagerness of joy to search for something you can *never* own until *you own you.* If you throw away what you have gained up to this present time to go and find a soulmate, you are headed for the pits of fire, I assure you, because you are not going forward; you are reacting backwards. You are wanting to go back to the virtue of primeval times, which is lost forever. You can *never* be who you were the first moment you looked into your eyes, the eyes of your other self that were a reflection of you. Too much water has gone under the bridge since then.

If you throw away what you have gained to go and find a soulmate, you are headed for the pits of fire, I assure you.

Contemplate this for a moment: When you looked into your mate's eyes, had you yet raped someone? Had you killed someone? Had you lived in decadence? Had you robbed someone? Had you thought you were soulless? Had you declared war on your neighbor?

Were you pious? Were you poor? Were you rich? Were you a whore? Were you a preacher? Were you confused?

Had you yet experienced death that moment you looked into your mate's eyes? Had you lived ten million years of lifetimes at that moment? Had you looked at your mate and saw only her breasts or his rear-end, like you do this day?

What were you looking at that first moment? A *virgin*, an *adventure*, but wholly without experience.

You can *never* go back to that splendid moment. It's long gone. Oh, the soul holds the virtue of that moment in memory; but you can never go back to it because the moment is *now*. You are too "smart"—and too limited—to have that innocence any longer. You must look at your souls *now*. Do you understand?

Audience: Yes.

Ramtha: Now, we are going to learn about how far you have come in regard to wisdom in your souls, so we can do away with your dogmas, get you out of the maze, and bring you back to center.

Know you entities that are called "extremists"? What think you extremists are? You don't know? So be it, I will send you an extremist!

You are all extremists. All of your moments, you live in one end of the spectrum or the other. When something "good" happens to you, you say, "That's positive." But know you what "positive" equates? Male gender. And when something "bad" happens to you, you term it "negative." Know you what negative is? Female. Now you know why you have had such a difficulty finding equality in genders.

Have you ever "allowed" something without judging it as good or bad, positive or negative, higher or lower? *Have you?* Have you ever seen something as just "is"? Well, it is only in

As long as you live in polarities, dogma will rule your life.

the consciousness called "is/be/allow" that you move beyond the extremities of negative/positive energy and out of judgment. As long as you live in polarities, dogma will rule your life. As long as there is "good," there must be always be "bad," because every moment you see something as good, you must create a "bad" to balance it. Did you know that? Whenever you embrace the understanding called "right," you will draw to you "wrong," the polarity of it. Now you know why things don't always "go right."

Are you ready for an eye-opener? Contemplate all of the cruddy things you've ever done. *(After brief pause)* Come on! When you do that, all of the grand things you've done will also come into your mind. (Don't you understand *how* this works?) So, contemplate crud—you know, all those things you do in your fantasies and all the things you did in your past. Did you ever rip the wings off a butterfly or trip another child and laugh? Those cruddy things.

(After pausing briefly to allow the audience to contemplate) Now, masters, you have been taught that God judges you. But God never has. Never! Man in the name of God *has* but not the Is. Did you know that if the Father, which is the All-in-All, had judged you for the least-little-cruddy thing you had done, you wouldn't exist in the next moment, and neither would life. The Is is without good and evil. It is without right and wrong. It is without perfection and imperfection. It is without negative and positive. God *is*. It is the isness of all that is, because it is everything that is existing. So if God had ever judged you, it would certainly have judged itself, for whatever you are, God is.

You have never been judged by God, the Is, Life. Only you have ever judged yourself. Know why? Because you call some things good and others bad. Get it?

Audience: Got it.

Ramtha: How would you live if you didn't have good or bad? Happily! *(Raises his glass)* To happiness!

Audience: To happiness!

Ramtha: There are those of you who do not want to give up

the premise of good and bad because if you do, it means you can no longer judge your neighbors, and you like doing that. If you give it up it means you can no longer see yourselves as better than others. Do you understand?

Now, there is another truth in regard to getting out of the maze and finding self: Whatever thought you allow to enter your brain, and you allow yourself to feel in your soul, manifests. That is why living with "right and wrong" is a great limitation—because it *divides* thought; it does not *allow* all thought to be received for an emotional knowingness. Are the lights coming on?

Before you can find your way through the maze, you must realize that judging thought is the thing that does not *allow* you to know; it *limits* the receivership of truth. That is why the words "be" and "allow" are wondrous words in your verbiage, because they bring forth an unjudgmental state of being that allows Superconsciousness, *unlimited mind,* to manifest.

Judging thought does not allow you to know. It limits the receivership of truth.

(*To the old pros*) We have talked of "center" before. Did you listen? Well, whatever you have judged since our last audience together, I am going to send back to you as messengers. I want you to re-evaluate your judgments. When you review them in a state of *being,* I am going to uplift the lot of you. Know you murk and mire and confusion? I'm going to raise you beyond that to another level, one that is joyful, for you will be in an understanding to see what I'm talking about. So be it!

Old Pros: So be it!

Ramtha: Now, for you: You can say you desire to do something; you can say you don't desire to do something. You don't have to feel it is either bad or good. Just go with your desires and do it! Understand?

Old Pros: Yes.

Ramtha: (Addressing the entire audience) Now, to God, all of you are the apple of his eye, for you are what God is. And God loves you, certainly, because what do you think holds you together, you *wretched* entities? (*Audience laughs.*) You know, you're only taking up space—and guess *whose* space it

When you get rid of right and wrong, you get rid of every dogma that was every created, and you find God in the process.

is? It is Love, called God, the cosmic glue that holds you together, the Is that allows you to experience whatever you contemplate in thought.

When you get rid of right and wrong, you get rid of every dogma that was every created, and you find God in the process. If you want to get out of the maze and the rut, if you are desiring to be God, to be without limitation, you must get rid of right and wrong and become judgeless. I will teach you how to be judge-less.

(Picks up his glass) This is a *lot* of drinking. But you *need* an ocean! *(Toasts)* To Life!

Audience: To Life!

Ramtha: Before you lie your pillow to your pallet and your head to your pillow, you will have judged three individuals. Now, you will probably say, "But master, I didn't *say* anything in regard to them!" But, you see, you don't *listen* so good. You can sit there and bite your lips and not let one word escape through them. But it's not what you *say,* it's what you think and embrace emotionally.

I will send your judgments back to you. What you think and feel in regard to another, so shall it be your destiny, straightaway! I will send it to you within a fortnight so that you learn to be without judgments. You're not going to learn to stop judging by someone *telling* you to do so. You are going to learn by becoming what you judge in another. So be it!

Now, what each of you sees in another will differ, perhaps, from your neighbor, but it all comes down to the same limited understanding. Very soon, after being knocked off your pedestal, having someone tell you off and slap one cheek and then the other, you're going to get the message. And know you who created that? Not *I;* I am simply sending your judgments home to you. *You* created it.

Experience teaches. How does a little child know that the fire is hot? When it pokes his fingers in the fire and he gets burnt. So, I will send you the runners of judgment. Bargain?

Audience: (Reluctantly) Bargain.

Ramtha: Not a lot of response on that one! *(Audience*

laughs.) I understand.

Now, heaven. You know, in heaven there's a very elitist staff. Only the goodie goodies go to heaven. But, masters, never desire heaven; desire knowledge. Knowledge *creates* that consciousness.

What is the result of mastering judgment? Do you know what utopia is? Well, you listen to your world reports, eh? You have a wondrous communication that gathers data, actions/reactions from all over your world—and it's very discouraging! But there was an hour on this plane when all things lived in harmonious movement and accord with one another, and it is coming again. But not before your plane goes through, very shortly, a rude awakening.

Your people are living in decadence. They are collapsing on a soul level. They are collapsing in their minds. They don't even know what it's like to be happy—and the lot of you don't know what it's like either!

A grand intimidation is coming upon your plane. The intimidation is from judgment and the polarity that judgment draws to itself. But when there is no longer the polarity of good and evil, right and wrong, you won't have negative/positive collision. You won't have war, you won't have peace; you will have only life. You won't have fear; you will have only life.

A grand intimidation is coming upon your plane. The intimidation is from judgment and the polarity that judgment draws to itself.

Now, I give a grand gift to the lot of you. For three days in your time you are going to live in Superconsciousness, for I will press it to you. You are going to know what it is like to live in a utopia that is without fear, that is noble and brilliant. You will have brilliance come to you and yet you will not be able to script it out, because how do you script a feeling? You will have health return. You will know what it is to look at others and see the faces of yourself. And the desire to judge them will not be there. That is what it is like when you have come to the center of negative and positive and have found Is. That is the wondrous prize of being and becoming.

For three days you will have a taste of utopia, of what is capable, and what *will* be upon this plane. So be it!

Audience: So be it!

Ramtha: Now, soulmates share their experiences. So, not only are you enriched with the endowment of all of *your* incarnations on this plane, but you are enriched with the shared wisdom of your other self who has become an individual, just like you are.

To tell you that not everyone here will find their soulmates comes as a relief to some of you, because you are not ready for yours. If you were to meet them in the tomorrow of your time but have done nothing to clean yourself up in order to find the relationship joyful, it would be an explosive, unmerciful relationship. Understand?

You women, your great limitation is the need to survive. Did you know that? You have an insecure passion that drives you, and you go after men with exuberant fervor. But you are still running around feeling that you've got to *prove* something to them, or you've got to *own* them.

All of you women want your soulmates, eh? You want the perfect lover, someone who can see you fat and ugly and still love you, someone to take care of you, to be there, to provide for you, to give you freedom. Well, I have something to tell you. There is no man on this plane at this hour who has reached godhood or knighthood to be that brave, that noble, that powerful and that unconditionally loving. They're in the same boat that you are, because they're looking for someone, just like you are—except you're not filling their bill any more than they are filling yours.

You came here wanting me to send you Mr. Wonderful? I won't do that. I want to show you *Mrs.* Wonderful.

Now, I desire for you to understand without "peaches and cream." You have always longed in your souls to be owned by someone and to copulate with someone. It is from seven and one-half million years of living for survival. You don't *There is more to life* know any better. You don't know that there is more to life *than simply bedding down* than simply bedding down with another entity. That is part of *with another entity.* the maze you live in. That is part of the hang-ups that you are riddled with.

Look at you! Have you looked at you lately? Why do you adorn yourselves? Is it because it makes *you* happy, or are you waiting to catch someone's eye? Do you ever go out into public affairs without painting yourselves up, adorning yourselves with gold and rubies, and decking yourselves out in heavy perfumes? I mean, *where* is the smell coming from? Why aren't *you* exuding it of your own *being?*

Now, I love you, but you are still wanting someone outside of you to fill up something you don't own *inside.* You are leaking! You have emotional holes, and you are leaking all over the place! The more bizarre you are the more leaky you are. That is a great truth. You don't like it? Sleep with it! You are trying to snatch someone to fill up what you don't have in here. That's why your relationships don't work out. You will *never* find what you are looking for because it doesn't exist.

You know, the blush is going to come off the rose very quickly once you get a wrinkle or two, once you begin to sleep around for a while and wake up to reality. The fantasy will begin to diminish. Because you are looking for something to fill a vacuum of polarization, you will only grow old and wretched, your teeth will fall out, your hair will become thin, you will get spots all over your body, you will be bent with age, and your fingers will not work properly. And no one will look at you then.

What about your soulmates? What are they feeling? The poor creatures are struggling for their *own* identity, and they are feeling humbly insecure because they are feeling all of these things from you.

Now, men! What are *you* looking for? Did you come to this audience because some woman who has had her eye on you coerced you into coming here? Are you looking for someone to balance out your madness, your brilliance? Are you looking for someone to take care of you? What are you looking for? You are also looking for someone to fill the emotional holes that you are riddled with.

Men!
What are you
looking for?

How many of you know how to cry? If you do, you have filled up great holes. But if you have set yourselves up to live

42

the ideals of social consciousness, I wish you to know that you will never achieve them.

Know you the dummy who lifts the bells? Know you that he is enslaved to them to keep "the look"? Because when he stops using them, know what happens to his rippling muscles? They turn to flab! And it's even more flabby than when he first started.

What are you enslaved to? What are you expecting your soulmates to do for you? To give you strokes? To make you feel like a man? You will *never* know what it's like to be a man until you can cry like a woman and be fearless like a soldier. You will never know what that is until you love all aspects of yourselves, and you don't. You cover yourselves up by being breadwinners, by being strong, by exuding a certain musk—whatever it is that you think is supposed to be masculine.

You will never know what it's like to be a man until you can cry like a woman and be fearless like a soldier.

And what about your penises? What are you going to do when you become impotent? Where are you going to put your idealistic form then? If you can't copulate or get an erection, what are you then? Hmm?

You are also filled with holes because you don't love what you are. You love an image that will only fade in time, and when it is gone you will have nothing there.

You don't know how to cry. You don't know how to say, "I'm afraid." You don't know how to walk away and be honorable. You don't know how to be anything other than *sexual*.

What are the lot of you looking for? Someone to make you feel all that you think you *aren't*?

Masters, wake up! As long as you have limited beliefs and limited minds, you're going to grow old, you're going to become impotent, you're going to have gnarled fingers and hair streaked with gray—and you are going to die. And what will you have done up till then? Chased an illusion.

Now, finding your soulmates. You draw your soulmate to you like great magnets when you begin to love yourself and fill the holes that you leak from so badly. When you can look into a grand mirror and love what you see—because you know your beauty is *unseen*—then you have filled the holes. When you can sleep at night without sleeping in terror, you have filled the holes. When you can walk through the marketplace and be *un*sexual, you have filled the holes. The more you plug them up and the more you are intimate with yourself, the closer you are to drawing this magnificent entity to you. And while you are loving yourself and becoming greater in your being, your soulmate is being uplifted. The knowledge is coming to your mate because the two you are the same soul and you share the wisdom.

Through the process of self-love, you become a christ. And when the christ has arisen within you, it quivers within your soulmate. It is two in the process of coming back to the immaculate One.

When the christ has arisen within you, it quivers within your soulmate.

(Picks up his glass and salutes the audience) I love you. I *love* you! So be it!

Audience: So be it!

Ramtha: Now, the next runner. I am sending you an immaculate mirror, a reflection with *no* holes, a reflection of you loving you. When you are insecure, when you are afraid, you are not loving you. So, I am sending you a vision that goes beyond this dream; and you will see yourself in the vision as a secure and fearless entity. So be it!

Some of you are still waiting for that mirror. Those of you who have seen the mirror, I will take you one step further. I'll show you a reflector that will mirror back every action of your brilliance. You have not seen such a mirror since first you became upon this plane, except this mirror is *heavy* with the treasure of wisdom. So be it!

(Surveys the audience, picks up his glass, and speaks in measured tones) It is enough this day. We have done great things. And you have a *host* of motley runners to contend with. *(Toasts)* To soulmates!

Audience: To soulmates!

Ramtha: That is all. I love you! So be it!

***

Saturday Morning Session
January 11, 1986

*Ramtha waits patiently on the stage while the audience re-
turns for the beginning of the second day's session. Quietly
stroking his face, like he did when he had a beard in his
lifetime, Ramtha observes the audience as they visit and talk.
After everyone has settled in their seats, he steps down from
the platform and begins to walk through the audience, occasionally stopping to speak to individuals. Ramtha walks up to
a man.*

Ramtha: (Kissing his hands) I am pleased you came to this
audience. *(Pointing to a crystal hanging around the man's
neck)* What be this?

Man: A crystal.

Ramtha: Why do you wear it?

Man: I was told that if I placed it close to my heart chakra
and energized it with self-love, the energy would stay with
me.

Ramtha: Know you what an amulet is? This that you are
wearing is an amulet. Know you that when you give power to
something to stabilize your power, you lose it yourself? Know
you that only *you* have dominion over you? Understand? For
adornment, it is lovely! But it is an enslavement.

(Walks over to a woman who has been taking notes) Can
you write down a feeling?

Woman: No.

Ramtha: Only reminders, eh?

*When you give power
to something
to stabilize your power,
you lose it yourself.*

Woman: I love you, Ramtha.

Ramtha: I am worth loving, master, but so be you.

Woman: Yes.

(Ramtha heads toward the platform, stopping occasionally to make eye contact with individuals in the audience. Upon returning to the platform, he proposes the first toast of the day.)

Ramtha: To a greater life! Forever, and ever, and ever! *(Bellows)* So be it!

Audience: So be it!

Ramtha: Drink heartily, sippers! *(Gulps the entire glass of water)* I love you. Indeed!

I am Ramtha the Enlightened One, your beloved brother; indeed, your beloved teacher. You have learned, you have absorbed, and you have come into a greater space of understanding. I salute you from the lord-god of my totality.

Now, there are those of you who insist on being unhappy. It is there to be seen. If you *want* to be unhappy, so be it! Know you what "want" is? *(Gets no response, so shouts) Do you?*

Audience: Yes!

Ramtha: You *should*. It's the most often used word used in your language. I know; I took a survey!

"Want" is what sets the wheels of manifestation into motion.

All of you want, want, want! Well, that is all right, because "want" is what sets the wheels of manifestation into motion.

Now, soulmates, hear this: I look at you and I see your lives. I see your hang-ups and hang-downs, your limitations, your predicaments, your illnesses, the coming of your illnesses, and I see who created them. You did. Everything that you are in this dream, you are because you *wanted* to be that way. Did you know that? Whether you are rich or poor, king or beggar, whether you are married, unmarried, seeking, secure, insecure, frustrated, you made it that way.

There are many of you who blame everything outside of you for your problems. Know you the dream? That everything in the dream—social consciousness, your parents, where you live, your government, your dog—is responsible for your unhappiness. Well, dreamers, you are the ones who are asleep, and you are the ones who will die.

To become sovereign is to realize that you created your life the way you wanted it. It wasn't your mother's or your father's fault for *anything* that happened to you! You chose them as parents for a vehicle of expression. You *chose* their genetic seeds—their sperm, their egg, the emotions in their chromosome structures. You picked the genetic clay to come through. What have they ever done but be who they are?

To become sovereign is to realize that you created your life the way you wanted it.

To bring back your power, to reclaim it, a master's first realization is that he created his own life and his own kingdom. He becomes *aware* that he chose everything. That awareness increases his power—brings it back home—and he is waking up from the dream. When you take responsibility and know that *everything* in your life, you created, you brought to you, that truth will set you free from guilt, blame, and hatred. It will bring peace home to you.

Many of you say you are "messed up" in your minds. Guess *who* messed you up? Take hold of the responsibility! It *belongs* to you. How do you unmess yourself? Want it! There is no psychology to mental health, only desire. There is not one problem that you have that cannot be changed in a twinkling of an eye. Not one. Not one!

A master wakes up from the dream and reclaims himself. Now, waking up *is* a very arduous process. But what do you want? Why are you here? You are here because you are wanting the unspeakable knowledge, unspeakable because those who are asleep in the dream will never realize it until they wake up, *feel* the knowledge, and then live it!

To master is to say, "I chose everything in my life for the experience of it. I have learned from it all. I have gained wisdom from the experiences of my life."

Know you that there is no such thing as a victim? *Harsh* teaching. But when good and bad are done away with, when life is seen as a continuum, an ongoing process, then there is no such thing as a victim; there is only life. The consciousness of "victim" creates the polarity called "pursuer."

Now, want. Everything that has happened to you, you *wanted* it to, for the end result called *emotional wisdom*. So it is not the games of *action* that have been important; it has been the treasure of *re*-action, which is called wisdom. And you've all gained it, except it hasn't fully become wisdom yet, because it's still clouded over by guilt and insecurity and blame and feelings of failure. When you bring the responsibility home and say, "I created it," then there is no longer such a thing as guilt or failure; there is achievement, there is wisdom. When you bring the responsibility for your life back home to you, you no longer blame your parents, your lover, your husband, your wife, your children, your dog, society, whatever. You can't hate any longer, for there is no object *outside* of you that creates the polarity of victim and pursuer, where you hate the pursuer because you feel you are a victim. You understand? When you take responsibility for your life, it eliminates those things. When you realize you created the dream, you are waking up, you are going home.

A master knows he is responsible for everything in his dominion. Know you what his dominion is? 'Tis his reality and life. A master is responsible for that. He is *not* responsible for humanity, only for himself. That understanding does away with leaders. It does away with priests and oracles and psychics. When you're a master, you never ask another for answers, because every moment you ask another for their advice, you remove yourself from knowingness. Now you know why a master walks alone.

Every moment you ask another for their advice, you remove yourself from knowingness. Now you know why a master walks alone.

A master *knows* his destiny, because a master possesses the power of the awakening christ. All he has to do is ponder and desire, and whatever he desires to know is revealed to him within a moment. Any time you follow someone else or you become a groupie or sect or cult, you give away that power; you are asleep.

You want to manifest? You want to turn water into wine? You want to manifest loaves of bread in your hand or gold in your treasury? As long as you follow, you can *never* do that! You will always be wanting "out here" because you have no power to make it happen in here! As long as you follow, as long as you seek answers "out there," you have lost the power to know, you have lost the christ; it doesn't quiver.

Every religion worships an unseen entity. This that I teach you is not a religion—and I am *definitely* not unseen; I am here and now. You are here to learn an unspeakable knowledge. You are here to learn of the love of God—which is not something "out there," beyond the moon or Alpha Centauri! That is not where God and heaven are! Heaven is within! God, the Father, the all-consuming light, is within you! You *are* that presence, that power, that beauty.

I address you as my brother, indeed my equal. The only difference between you and me is that I *know* who I am and you don't! You have been in ignorance for seven and one-half million years, because that's how long you've been enslaved to dogma and fear.

Look! *(Sighs and shakes his head)* You can't even cure a simple headache! *(Tugs several times at a rose in the floral arrangement and finally yanks it free)* I don't give up! *(Audience laughs and applauds.)*

You hear the term "master," but you really don't know what it means. You imagine it is one who lives in a cave, wears a sackcloth and ashes, and doesn't look anyone in the eye lest he gets their vibrations! That is another dogma, another powerless pretense, and you've all been pretending for a very long time.

Know you what some of you are going to do with this teaching? You're going to run amuck and ask other teachers where your soulmates are. And they'll tell you that they have the answer, except it won't be the truth, and you'll never find your mates. Nor will you ever know what it is to heal yourselves or to see the glimmer beyond this dimension, because you're not sovereign.

My audiences are not to create a following. If I desired to be worshiped I would not teach you the unspeakable truths, nor would I manifest for you, nor would I tell you what you are and exalt what you are. I would keep you in ignorance and take away your power. And my audience would be as vast as the world. Did you know that? Because I *am* that powerful!

49

You have been in ignorance for seven and one-half million years, because that's how long you've been enslaved to dogma and fear.

But I do not need worship. I already *am* God! I already *own* forever! What do I want from *you?* Can you give me more of forever? Hardly!

This that I do, I do simply because I love you. For when one comes into the absoluteness of what one is, one sees the whole of All-in-All and becomes all that is within the All.

I desire for you to be a light to the world. Your plane needs it. You are approaching epic moments, and few are going to see the grandness of the other side. I desire for you to learn the greatest knowledge, but you can learn it only when you are ready for it. You have to be awake to listen. You have to be awake to see the runners and the miracles when they manifest. You have to be sovereign. Sovereign! When you follow, you learn only to follow and you lose your power; you are leaking energy everywhere. Did you know that?

You wanted to find the greatest teacher. I *am* the greatest teacher, in my reality. I have no difficulty telling you that. But the greatest teacher to *you* is the god within you that makes you "you." Understand? I am a grand mirror of great virtue and truth, of impeccable genius and knowledge. When you see all of that in me, it means you also possess it within yourself. Do you understand? A master sees, reclaims, and be-comes. Be-comes! What are you becoming? You are becoming *free*. To become that, you don't have to *be* anything in particular; you only have to *be*. That is owning *all* of the power and allowing.

You have to *want* to be a master. You have to *want* it. Know you how you wanted everything else? Fame, fortune, beauty, lovers, clothing, hovels, gold, silver, myrrh. Know you how you wanted all those things? It's the *same* want. If you put the *same* power behind wanting to be a master as you have done for tedious, petty things in the dream, you'll become the all-wise knowing intelligence.

In my life, I *wanted* it. I didn't know what it was I wanted, I just wanted it. And, perhaps, the grandest manifestations come from the imageless want.

There are some of you who are terribly unhappy. I see it in

you. Well, I have no pity for you because I see, in a grander understanding, you set it up, you wanted it that way. You want to feel the way you are feeling. Only when you *want* it to be different will you change. Nothing, no one, no power, not even I, with all of the runners and the miracles and the knowledge, can change your stubborn minds. Because, you see, the key to the door of understanding is on *your* side of the door. You are a god, and whatever you desire for your kingdom, so it is! That grand and only law can never be disputed or overridden. You understand?

Audience: Yes.

Ramtha: Some of you are not going to get this teaching because you like judging other entities. You are bound by your bigotry, you are bound by your superstitious minds, and you are bound by good and evil—because you *want* to be! And you want to be seen as the victim so you can succor after pity from others. I allow you to do that. 'Tis your will, so dream on! But you will dream right to your grave.

For those of you who are awakening, all that you are learning, you are beginning to feel in your souls; and your mates, wherever they are, are beginning to have quivers of this grand teaching. Something inside them is wanting. They don't know what it is, but they are beginning to feel grander about themselves. They don't know why, but they are. You are sharing the emotion with them. So, the souls of your soulmates are getting this understanding now, and they are waking up. And very shortly, for no reason, they will understand that they are responsible for their lives, and that truth will set them free. Free! To fly away like a bird? Not necessarily. But to be free of dogma, the intimidator of "expansive mind." They are waking up because of you. They are *re*acting on their end; and every moment they are reacting, you are getting *their* intensity. So, you're getting two for the price of one! Get it? Because the two of you share *everything*. Even if you have never seen one another since first you split, you have always shared everything.

Now, all along, you thought that because you had such a

Nothing, no one, no power, not even I, with all of the runners and the miracles and the knowledge, can change your stubborn minds.

52

fancy for Egyptian artifacts, you must have lived there. And you went to a seer, and he told you of a very elaborate life that you lived there (Know you elaborate life? You were a queen or a pharaoh. No one was ever a peasant in the street. It's not a nice thing to tell a customer!)—only to find out that you never lived there at all! Your *soulmate* lived there! Understand?

Why don't you particularly want to go to Mesopotamia? Because you already *lived* in Mesopotamia and spent grand lifetimes there. You don't have a draw to it because you gained everything you wanted from that experience. It's old business, it's old hat. But your soulmate will have a knowingness of Mesopotamia within them, and yet it is a mystery why they feel that, because they've never been there. It's because they've reaped the benefits of *your* exhausting lifetimes! See how it works?

To awaken the master within you is also to quiver the christ within your soulmate.

To awaken the master within you is also to quiver the christ within your soulmate.

Now, I am endeavoring to teach you an unteachable knowingness that comes only from *want*. You can practice the virtue of being judgeless, you can practice the virtues of mercy and grace, but you'll never be a polished isness until you *want* to be, until you wake up!

(Puts his hands on his hips) You know, I'm like a baby-sitting service! I baby-sit you a grand amount. I keep sending reminders back to you, hoping that you'll get out of this pickle. It only takes a moment to want that—and that moment is aligned *wholly* within you! You don't have to chant until you're hoarse. You don't have to meditate. You only have to be. Then those virtues just are. They just *are*. And the closer you are to a living thing of nature, the grander that "being" will become. Then your genius will flow.

Have you looked at a flower lately? Have you smelled its aroma, its deep perfume? Have you marveled at its color, its life? If you haven't, you haven't marveled at the reflection of the genius, the god, that is within you.

You don't have to do a single ritualistic practice to become. You only have to *want* to become and to love God, to *love*

God, with all of your might and all of your being and all of
your breath, because the breath that you take *is* God, the Life
Force. And don't tell me that you love God if you still judge
your neighbors, because your neighbors *are* God. They are
God! Do you understand?

Audience: Yes.

Ramtha: Now, we make a little toast. *(Picks up his glass)*
To the awakening master. To Life! Forever and ever! So be it!

Audience: So be it!

Ramtha: Now, joy. All of you are thinking that your soulmate will bring you joy. That's why you want them, lickety-
split! But that is another limitation, because you are still looking for someone outside of you to make you happy, *aren't*
you? A soulmate is *not* going to bring you happiness! Oh! did
I see faces fall on the ground! When the passion and the explosion thereof ceases, it's still going to be the same old *you*, except sort of amplified.

Joy is *self*-realized, and it draws your power back to you.
Did you know that? Joy is the result of sovereignty. It is the
great treasure, the paradise of feeling. And yet there are a host
of you here who have *never* known that feeling. You have
known the burst of laughter from crude jokes and the like, but
you have never been lifted and happy at all moments because
you are living in a state of being. There is always something
that brings you down—and you create those things yourselves. If your children make you unhappy, that's because you
have allowed them to. If your husband doesn't please you,
that's because you have made it that way. You have allowed
all of your happiness to be found through *them* rather than
through *you*. Get it? Anything that doesn't make you happy,
you give your power away to, because you allow *it* to determine your *re*-action. Did you know that? You depend on
everyone else to make you happy. That is how weak you are!
You even depend on your loins to make you happy, and that is
being unfair to you.

A master always *is*. A master loves, certainly, and his love
is unconditional, but he also holds on to himself, because the

53

*A soulmate is not
going to bring you
happiness!
Oh! did I see faces
fall on the ground!*

more he holds on, the greater is his healing power to the entire world.

You become God and christ *for yourself*—in spite of the world yet *for* the world. In other words, *you come first*—you and your god. The rest of the world will just have to wait until the process of becoming is "just wonderful."

Look at you! Know how many people you depend upon to make you happy? Would you like a closer look? I will send them to you—all of them! And they're all going to come a'running, and they're all going to ask your advice—but they're going to do the *opposite* of what you tell them to do! And they're going to be there, seemingly, all at once. All the people you have forced to make you happy are going to be on you like *glue!* At first, you are going to feel important and wonderful, but when they don't do *anything* you tell them, you'll become angry, miserable, unhappy. I do this so you cannot fool yourselves any longer. I want you to realize that you are depending upon other people to make you happy rather than yourselves.

Ask yourselves, "Would any of these individuals die for me when it comes time for me to pass from this plane?"

I want you to ask yourselves, "Would any of these individuals die for me when it comes time for me to pass from this plane?" Now, I want you to *think* about this. Of all these important people who you are so busy living for and making them bring you your joy, will any of them die in your place to spare you the trouble? Would you like a runner to find out? Would you like to come to the moment of passing this plane and see what their reaction will be when you ask them, "Will you trade places with me?" Do you want me to go that far?

Audience: No.

Ramtha: Why not? *(Audience laughs.)* You are 'fraidy-cats, another limitation.

Masters, they won't take you up on the offer. They *won't.* So why are you making them the key to your happiness? Why are you making them responsible for your lives? They don't deserve it. And you're being an enslaver! Did you know that? Well, it is a great truth that no one has really taught you, because it is a threatening way to see life. The lot of you don't want to hear that because you are not ready to be sovereign. That is why you are not ready for your soulmates—because that is what it takes: to be happy *all by yourself.* Indeed? *Do you hear me?*

Audience: Yes!

Ramtha: Do you *feel* me?

Audience: Yes!

Ramtha: I'll test you! So be it!

Perhaps you are beginning to feel a picture of the imminent flow which is simple, which is the "within process" that allows the brain to grow, that allows the light to become enormous around you.

Now, to take back your power, ask only yourself for advice. Remember, no one else knows the answer greater than the god within you knows, because the question *is* the answer. From the lord-god of your being, ask the Father within you for knowingness, and it will manifest it for you—and it's all customized! From the lord-god of your being, ask the Father within you for clarity, for knowingness, and then just be and allow it to come. When you least expect it, you will be illuminated. Illuminated! You will know the answer beyond words; it is wisdom now in your soul, another pearl to take home with you. And you'll begin to feel rather arrogant when you begin to know.

Now, because you know for *yourself* does not mean that you know for your neighbor. It is dangerous to give knowingness to others. Know why? Because if they are not engaged in becoming, they want to hear only what they want to hear. And when it doesn't work, guess who they are going to look up?

I have been talking to you individually, but I have been really talking to *two* of you. ('Tis a grand, unlimited way to spread this audience.) All I have told you will come to pass for the glory of the Father within *you* and the other "you" that you are, to give forth a revelation of truth so that you will be free.

Now, another great teaching you should know: There is no such a thing as *un*truth. In the All-in-All, there is no such

55

You are not ready to be sovereign. That is why you are not ready for your soulmates— because that is what it takes: to be happy all by yourself.

thing as *un*-All. Everything is true, because whatever one thinks, he feels; and whatever is felt has become a reality. A person can change his truth any moment, for whenever one changes his mind he changes his feelings. And if his feelings are changed, he has taken on a new truth, and he will react differently. Did you know that? Didn't know that, eh?

Everyone is right. The person who does not believe in God is right. The person who *hates* you is right. Did you know that? Because everyone is a god, and they create their own reality, thus their own truth. These are staunch teachings, but a master understands.

There are those who think they have *the* truth (it is called a dogma); and if you do not believe their truth they will persecute you, ostracize you, and condemn you in the name of God. Did you know that they are right? Their truth is a reality—but only if you *accept* it.

If you desire to become One, you must allow others their truth. If you do not, then you become involved in their polarity; you become a warrior. Do you understand? If you do not allow them their truth, without persecution, without warring upon them, you will never know your own, and you will be enslaved to your judgments of others. Giving your power away is also done by condemning others for what they believe. Understand?

Audience: Yes.

Ramtha: Now, what does it mean "to be a light"? It means *living* your truth, *your* reality. Truth is not a *speakable* thing, it is a *livable* thing. And the virtues that go along with being a light are "loving in freedom" and "allowing." When you love others by allowing them the freedom to hold and express their own truths, you are a light to those who *want* to see your truth. Do you understand how it works? (*Picks up his glass and speaks in a somber tone*) To freedom.

Audience: To freedom.

Ramtha: Now, I will send you your next runner. I will send you three entities. The entities who will come to you will have different faiths, and they will each persecute the others' faith because they feel only they have the "right" one. And they will be *very* persuasive. I will send them to you, and I want to see and feel your reaction to the three and what difference you make to them. Bargain?

Audience: Bargain.

Ramtha: So be it!

(Looking the audience over) A wonderful thing is happening. There are some of you who are getting it. And as you are getting it your soulmate is getting it.

Now, before I allow you to go to your latrines, there is a small teaching I desire to give you in regard to "spiritual truths," because there are many of you here who call yourself "spiritualists," don't you? Did you know that that's a limitation? Did you know that if you say you are a spiritualist, you have given your power away to another illusion? Because *everything* is spiritual; there isn't *one* thing that isn't.

Spiritualists have their own dogmas:

If you say that you believe in karma, you are giving your power away and setting your destiny in stone.

If you say that you believe in sin, then you are doomed, certainly. If you believe that the wheel-of-life, reincarnation, is the utopia of continuous living, you are of limited mind—because there is more beyond the wheel, such as you cannot imagine!

If you believe in "twin souls," you have a limited truth. There are only soul*mates*.

To say you are part of a "soul family" is to commit yourself to the same old souls without the exploration of the human drama in all of its beauty.

To say you are part of a "soul group" is to eliminate all of your brothers and make you an "archy." Know you an "archy"? You know, *higher*archy. When you become selective in groups, you are hierarchies, you are altered, because groups are a part of altered ego.

Know you that "ego" means your identity, which is God. Do you know what "altered ego" is? *Altered* identity, *altered* God, which equates limited expression, limited god, one-third brain power. Know how you can tell that you have a powerful altered ego? You are riddled with prejudice and judgments, you live for social consciousness . . . and you can't even heal a simple headache.

Now, "possessive" spirits. There are those who believe in possessive spirits; it has become their religion. But there are no such entities. You can only be possessed by your own altered ego. You can call it a name, you can call it Satan, but, in reality, it is you. There is no force beyond the seen that is evil. Evil exists only in the minds of those of flesh and blood. There is no thing in the unseen that can possess you or take you over. Only you can do that.

Some of you, particularly those of you in the "archy" class, have "multudious" guides—and they're always aristocrats! And the more guides you have, the more special you feel you are. Well, that is a dogma; it is a spiritual dogma.

Do you know *who* your guides are? You! A-w-w-w. *(Audience laughs.)* You do not have to agree with me. You can hang on to those entities if you want to. It is all right. But if you start asking guides for answers, you are giving away your power, aren't you? In the grandest knowingness, if you are a sovereign god, you don't *need* a guide—especially forty-two of them!

If you are a sovereign god, you don't need a guide—especially forty-two of them!

Your spirit is the god of your being. It is the light that surrounds your body. It was the first light of creation and it is called the blue corona. Your scientists have photographed this wondrous entity, so it is a scientific fact. But your photography has been able to capture only the lower electrum of the blue corona, because there it is negative/positive energy; it is electricity at that part. So you have been seen around your body. And yet the god of your being goes beyond sight. Your photography is not swift enough to capture the greater light, the higher frequency of the blue corona, which goes very far out. For one who is a master, his light can be nigh three miles in diameter. To one who is close-minded and collapsing internally, the light is very close to his body because he is heavy in material density. He is not en*light*ened.

The god of your being is the light that holds you together. If you did not have that grand light around you, you would dissipate and float off into knowingness, cell by cell. So, what is it that keeps you together? What is the glue? It is called *love*. It is Thought, which is God, in the form of light.

Oftentimes entities will see their own spirit, their own god, walking in front of them, and they think it is another entity. They even give it a name. And yet it is only the light of their beings, because often your light will focus in front of you and you'll get glimmers of it.

You and your god, which has taken on many names, is your great guide. That's where you get all of your answers. So rather than calling it Chief Redfeather, or Dr. Ming Hing Poo of the Third Dynasty, or George, call it what it is: I Am! It *does* know *everything*.

Everyone who starts hearing a voice in his head immediately thinks he is a channel or a medium. He is not. Why can't you accept that it is your *own* knowingness, because *that* is what you are hearing. When you ask yourself, the god of your being, it *knows;* it has the answers. When you ask someone else, it's always a fruitless game, a riddle, a speculation.

Know you what an amulet is? It is a special emblem worn around the neck that is supposed to be endowed with the power to protect, uplift, heal, and keep you in line. Know you that crystals are amulets? Did you know that they are also a limitation, because what outside of your being can make you greater in your being, eh? It is all right to have crystals splayed across your body, but if you are rotten inside, it ain't gonna make any difference! And a crystal cannot heal you. It cannot. Only *you* can do that.

A crystal cannot heal you. Only you can do that.

Stars and planets do not govern your life. It is a hypocrisy to say that you are God and then say that the universe has planned your destiny. Know you why astrology works? Because there are those who *believe* it into working. They are *that* powerful! And yet they give credit to the stars. They should say, "I did it!" and it would be a most proper acknowledgement. Are you getting the picture?

Audience: Yes.

60

Ramtha: No thing outside of you governs you unless you want it to. You have entities tell you what *you* know, and then you give *them* all the credit! You are giving your power away to them, to the stars! to the amulets! to the crystals! You cannot balance your chakra system with crystals! Wake up. *(Screams) Wake up!* No wonder the gurus have had a field day in your country! *(Shakes his head in mock disgust)* No wonder! You don't even *need* to balance your chakras, didn't you know that?

Your seals, your chakras, are the divine seven that were in the beginning of the human drama and the split of soulmates. They allowed and created the flow of hormones that evolved according to whether there was a positive or negative energy within the body. The seals you now possess connect with the seals of your soulmate. Did you know that? They are one and the same; they just work off of different energy. They are connected, and they are trading truths. So what do you need to balance them for? They are *all* operational. If they weren't, you wouldn't be here.

Now, you think sticking little needles in your body is going to bring you a revelation? Dream on! 'Tis another dogma. It is all right to give power to the practice, but you have also given away your knowingness. Did you know that?

Now you understand why so many entities do not love me —because I kick away their crutches.

(Picks up his glass, sighs, and toasts) To the human comedy! *(Looks at all the gloomy faces and explodes with laughter at their seriousness)*

As long as you believe in a power outside of you, you'll never become a christ. Never!

Those are all spiritual dogmas. And it's all right to believe in them if that's your truth. It is all right. But as long as you believe in a power outside of you, you'll never become a christ. Never!

Dogma is a hypocrisy to divine inner revelation. It cannot exist unless you take the power away from yourself and put it into something else. Then it becomes dogma and a religion.

You will never be able to ascend having so many notes payable. You will never ascend having so many spiritual debts scattered around. You will only die. Ascension is the natural reaction to a life lived in joy as a *sovereign* entity. The more power you take back, the happier you are going to be and the more your brain opens up. The more your brain, your receiver, opens up, the greater your body becomes. When your brain is in full bloom, liken unto a lotus blossom, you can ascend, because you have the *power* to raise the vibratory frequency of your cellular mass and go into another time, another place, another dimension—because you own it *all*. Do you understand what I have taught you this morning in your time?

Audience: Yes.

Ramtha: Now, get happy. Get happy! My beloved masters, if you contemplate what I teach you here, follow your feelings, and allow yourselves to be, you will soon find that hate and bitterness and anger are within you no more. And in the vacuum will be joy, the healer of the spirit. And those holes that you sort of leak out of? They will have been plugged up, because you now own *all* feelings. You will have realized that you've always had the power to experience the feelings you thought only someone else could give you. And that is when you're going to draw right to your doorstep that mystical enigma called your soulmate, because then you *deserve* each other, for you are both in ownership of the only law that governs life: I Am! When you own that sovereignty, that feeling of joy, no thing, not even death, can ever remove that from your beauteous selves.

Get happy! Get rid of the things in your life that do not bring you joy. You *know* what they are. All you have to do is look around you. What enslaves you? What limits you? What is around you that pushes your buttons? No matter how much it costs, allow them to flow from your life.

Look at your walls. What do you hang there? What do you read? What are you filling yourself with? *Anything that doesn't bring you joy, get rid of it!* It's liken unto a leech! If you are not happy in your relationship, say so! Be honorable; live your truth. For the first time, *live your truth*. If you want

*Ascension is
the natural reaction
to a life lived
in joy
as a sovereign entity.*

to move, move! What is stopping you?

Don't do anything that doesn't bring you joy. If you do, that is not loving you. Be fair with yourself. Do what brings you joy, in spite of everyone else. Do it for the sake of God within you. Go for it!

Now, another spiritual dogma. Know you "The Path"? In religion it is so narrow (because narrow-minded entities created it), not everybody can get on it—not even them!

The path to enlightenment is not *one* path. The path is right wherever you are.

Do you know that your path can wind, go over hills, through dales and glens, pass through sleepy hollows, cross rivers and oceans and babbling brooks? Know you that it can go under the sea, over the sea, or perhaps to the other side of the moon? How will you know if you are on the right path? When you've got a smile on your face; when what you're doing makes you *happy*. The right path is wherever you are happy. And if the path has a fork in the road and you have an option, and neither one makes you happy, and you're confused, do not make a decision. Do not! Stand there with a smile on your face, right where you are, and allow the confusion to subside. It won't take a century, only moments.

Never make a decision when you are confused. Allow the answer to come. When you *allow* it, the path will become clear because it will *feel* good. It may not be right for others, but it will be for you. Understand?

Audience: Yes.

Ramtha: Happiness is the only path to enlightenment. Because the more you do what brings you joy, the greater your receiver opens up. And the more you are gratifying you, the closer you are to God. That is all it takes.

Now, know you what boredom is? There are a lot of you who are bored! You feel it in here. Boredom is the language of the soul saying you have gained everything from that experience. It no longer intrigues you, challenges you, or uplifts you, because you have learned what you needed to learn from it. You'll always know when it's time to move on to another

*How will you know
if you are on
the right path?
When you've got
a smile on your face;
Happiness
is the only path
to enlightenment.*

experience, because when you have learned enough from where you're at, you'll become bored. This is applicable to labor, to creativity, to relationships, husbands, wives, lovers. It is applicable to everything! If you are bored with something, it's time to change; it's time to move on. The master knows he has gained, so he moves on. And he goes only in the directions that bring him joy. He gains, and he moves on. Now, you can live in the same old hovel for the rest of your life and be completely happy there. If it makes you happy, stay there. Do you understand?

Audience: Yes.

Ramtha: Now, what is the voice of God? What is that knowingness that you were thinking would come from the heavens like a bolt of lightning and tell you what to do? It is *feelings.* The voice of God is *feelings.* To hear the voice of God is to listen to what you feel. In feeling, indeed, *is* the unspeakable knowledge. Now you know why I cannot teach you that knowingness—because *you* are the ones who must feel it! I can *tell* you of that feeling, but you will never understand what I am talking about until *you* experience it, until you feel it. Do you understand now?

(Toasts) To boredom! To change! To the future!

Audience: So be it!

Ramtha: Know you why you are so unhappy? Because you are afraid to change; you are scared to venture into anything that isn't familiar. That's why you are bored, miserable, unhappy, wretched, suicidal creatures! Did I sum it up?

Contemplate it for a moment. Are you stuck with the same old lover? Are you living in the same dull place? Are you working the same monotonous job? Yet, you do not change because you are afraid. But did you know that there is no thing in the future "nows" that is fearsome? Nothing.

I recently gave an audience prophecies of the days to come. I told them to prepare themselves—to do what has *always* been a traditional way of existence in nature. I told them to gather foodstuffs and put them away liken unto an ant. Have you ever watched an ant? If you haven't I'll send you to an ant mound. It's a grand teaching, because even though they have enough to eat they are *also* putting foodstuffs away. Why? Because they know the season is changing and winter is coming.

I said unto this audience, "Go and prepare for yourselves a two-year supply of food. Two years." I said unto them that the shadows of Superconsciousness and the graveness of social consciousness were coming—and they took it out of context and became fanatics! They immediately took it as a dogma rather than the natural thing to do, and they thought that anyone who didn't do likewise was foolhardy. They wanted to see an end come to social consciousness, but they had chosen parts of the teaching to see only *one* way for it to happen. And yet there are *many* ways.

All of you should exhibit the knowledge of the creatures that you created. Have you lost the knowingness to be prepared? It does not *mean* preparing for the world to end! It means there may be a long winter on the land. But, certainly, when winter falls, spring is not too far ahead. Get it?

You think I suppress knowledge from you? I do. Know why? Because you can't handle it all. You are not ready to know many things because you still look at the future with a suspicious, fearful mind. Until you can make a change from boredom into happiness, you are not *ready* to know all that is coming forward.

You are not ready to know many things because you still look at the future with a suspicious, fearful mind.

Nature, which is God, the rhythm of life, if you will, is refining itself. It is getting rid of those things that do not propagate, that do not add to the value of life. It is getting rid of those things that are warring against the patterns of evolution.

The diseases that I spoke about long ago are now here. No one knew what I was talking about when I said they would happen. But they are nature getting rid of those who do not add to the patterns of evolution.

Know you what an earthquake is? It is the movement of your earth. It is like a zipper. Know you a zipper? Hmm? The crust of your planet has many of them so that it can move. But know you what dumbbells you are? You build your hovels on top of the zippers! And then, when they quake, you say it is an act of vengeance from nature that has destroyed everything. It is *your* stupidity! It's like building your house on top of a volcano so that you have a better view. Well, you'll get a view such as you have never known before. It is called being blown to kingdom come.

The earth has to move, just like you do. That is its natural thing to do. That is why there will always be quakings in the earth and volcanic movement.

Know you what the volcanoes are? They are steam valves. Your earth is hollow on the inside. There is pressure that builds between the outer and inner layers of the crust, and it must have release. When they blow, they let off the pressure at the zipper.

Now, there are dead volcanoes. They have been used for eons as "doors" by entities who live within the center of your earth. But there are also many volcanoes that are sleeping dragons.

There are zippers close to your coastal lines. If you are going to build your very expensive hovels upon them, know that you are committing suicide. You may blame it on God or the revolt of nature, but it is not *nature* destroying you; it is *you* who are limited in your brain who are doing that.

Look at all of the land masses where there is no one living. There is plenty of room for everyone without having to live on top of zippers! There you can create your own paradise, your own sea, your own ocean, if you want to.

It is not Nature destroying you; it is you who are limited in your brain who are doing that.

You know, I enlighten entities, and yet they run around like scared chickens! That is why when I speak of the future, I speak of it with great integrity.

Simply know that you are going into a winter, and be prepared for it. But also know that spring will soon follow. Do you understand?

Audience: Yes.

Ramtha: Now, change. You are afraid to change. So what I am going to do is, I'm going to manifest for you every boredom in your life until you are in manic depression. It often takes too much of something to get you to look at it.

(Audience groans.)

Masters, on one level you are wanting this.

Now, the next manifestation I am sending you is a brilliant door. Brilliant! You will have a choice. You can stay in your depression or you can go through the door. You will not know what is on the other side of the door, but it is called the future. I will manifest the door for you but you must make the decision. Bargain?

Audience: Bargain.

Ramtha: So be it!

Now, I will also manifest all of your fears. I will manifest them because they are dark things. Now "darkness" does not equate evil; dark means that they are hidden from the light. Know you why they are dark? Because they are unknown; and whatever is unknown, your survival instincts tells you to be suspicious and fearful of. I will bring all of your fears right to your doorstep so that you may have knowledge of them and own them. *Own* them. It is a part of mastery. Masters, once you own them, what will you be afraid of thereafter? Nothing. *No thing.*

What is happening to your soulmates through all of these manifestations? They are having *their* fears come forward and they are resolving them. And what they resolve in their being, you gain from.

So, now you are beginning to gain a wisdom and a knowingness and a fearlessness that you never had before. And though your soulmate is not quite sure what's going on in its life, whatever it is, it is quite marvelous. Your soulmate will intuitively react to your actions, and it will begin to have a cache of provisions. It will do this naturally. And when it goes through the actions, it gives you the support to feel good about what *you* are doing. So, you're growing together. Understand? Whatever you do, you are doing for the two of you, the *totality* of yourself.

Whatever you do, you are doing for the two of you, the totality of yourself.

You have been given grand teachings, and I have hard-pressed them to you. You will be even more hard-pressed when you leave this audience. You will be pressed into your masterhood—because you *want* to be! The knowingness that would have taken you a million lifetimes to gain, you are gaining in moments. I salute you for allowing that to occur.

Now, go and have lunch. Eat heartily. Drink a tea with your lunch, not milk. I am not desirous of you to come back here and fall asleep. Whenever you eat and accompany it with milk (which you all need), the body becomes lethargic. Drink only water or tea with your meal so that you are alive when you come back here. Because if you are a lethargic audience, I will send you to rest. Bargain?

Audience: Bargain.

Ramtha: When the hour reaches half-past the one, return. Indeed?

Contemplate your splendid selves. Bless your food; it will do wonders for your body. So be it! That is all.

***

Saturday Afternoon Session
January 11, 1986

After all attendees have returned from lunch and are seated, Ramtha begins the session with a toast.

Ramtha: To becoming!
  Audience: To becoming!
  Ramtha: To Life! Forever, and ever, and ever! So be it!
  Audience: So be it!
  Ramtha: Know you what a "cram course" is? Well, this is a cram course, indeed. How much you get from it is how much you open up and allow.

  Now, you are sitting here on your rumps, filled and rested (some, a bit lethargic), and you are wondering, "Am I making progress?" You are, indeed. Because knowledge must be embraced before the manifestation of it can be seen. You are like vessels into which wine is being poured. When you are full and fervent, mellow, enriched and ruby, your destiny will be sweet indeed.

  Sitting right where you are, you are absorbing like a master absorbs. Know you that when others are seeking fame, fortune, and notoriety, and they are hard-pressed to manifest these experiences in a polarity understanding—in limited thought—a master can sit and contemplate the concept of them, embrace the feeling within his soul, and gain all the wisdom from those experiences—without ever moving from his pallet! Did you know that?

  A master can own the wisdom without having to experience

Knowledge must be embraced before the manifestation of it can be seen.

it through a three-dimensional understanding.

You are embracing knowledge right where you are. You are owning it, blow by blow, and it is becoming a grand emotional reality rather than a dry philosophy, a conjecturous concept, if you will. I am very pleased, for even the most closed-minded of your lot is being stirred. That is progress; that is ev-o-lu-tion.

Now, I said to you that everyone has a soulmate. Did you know that your *cat* has a soulmate? Did you know that your doggie has a soulmate? They all have soulmates. How does Phoo-phoo know it belongs to another dog? Well, how do they know their own kind? You say, "instinct." Of course, but what is instinct? It is cellular soul memory. This, perhaps, will put some entities down, because they want to have exclusive rights to soulmates. But all life-forms in mass that take on negative and positive energies have opposites. It is the science of the three-dimensional plane.

Now, there is much more to teach you about the poignant destiny of soulmates. There is much more that it encompasses, for "soulmates" is the sharing of all of life's experiences. So there are a myriad of elemental experiences that have greatly affected you and your soulmate, or your other self, and we will expound on them. We are going to get down to the nittus-grittus of some of them.

Know you what a "crossover" is? I will explain:

When the soul of a woman is in a woman's body the seals are in harmonious movement; they are aligned. When a male energy is in a male body the seals are aligned; the hormonal flow is in balance, harmonious balance.

Man in his drama and in his dream has, for many reasons, come from the beginning of virgin mind into the depths of decadence. The downfall of the divinity of mankind occurred when man proclaimed women "soulless." The reason for this? When God, or a soul, is taken out of you, you have no power; you are a no thing, a no one; you are less than the animals in the street. The clever entities who do this, do so because they can then use you for their own desires, their own

The downfall of the divinity of mankind occurred when man proclaimed women "soulless."

privileges, their own wants, and make you do their bidding.

Women once had status equal to men. Men and women used to share equal power. When the king and queen were on the throne, they would take confidence in one another, sharing their wisdom, opinions, and views. But long ago in your history, a very powerful prophet so desired to have rulership over people, that in the name of God he brought forth a new teaching: women were soulless and were subordinate to men.

Women, in the name of God, were made to step down from their equality with men, and they became like herded animals. Even your holiest teachings from ancient times tell of "divine" men, each possessing many wives, giving their wives away, lying with others to create sons—and *that* was considered "holy"!

There has been a lot of speculation about the most devastating thing that ever happened to mankind. Many of you will think of your recent history and the murder of millions by an entity who had them put to their deaths. But there were sieges long ago that you don't even know of that put many *more* to their deaths. And yet all of those together would not be as great a travesty as the one called the "fall of women," because from that time, women became pleasure objects for men. They were herded like cattle into harems. They were sold on the auction block in the marketplace under silken awnings of bright orange and lemon-yellow. The sound of squawking geese and the smell of garlic, old cheese, rotted wine, and camel dung, penetrated your senses as naked women stood in review, painted in kohl and henna, waiting to go to the highest bidder. It happened all of the time.

What began to happen is that women did not desire to have girl children, for they would be exalted in survival only if they bore sons. Sons were the demand because they fed the war machine. Oftentimes a little girl of only thirteen years of age would bear forth a girl child in silent agony, and for the sake of her own survival she would fling it onto the dung heap outside the city walls, where hyenas and coyotes would tear it from limb to limb. An unmerciful death indeed. (Remember,

*Women,
in the name of God,
were made to step down
from their equality
with men.*

every emotion was being recorded in the soul.)

No one thought anything of marketing off little girls, who by the time they were three years of age had had their purity broken with a marble phallus so that the satrap who had purchased them for his harem could molest them. When the little girls began to mature they would find themselves wrapping their breasts to keep them flat, and plucking the hairs from their private places so they would always look like little girls—because once they were past thirteen years of age, they were considered old and undesireable. Did you know that? No one wanted entities in his harem who could bear children.

Women were not permitted to be educated. It was forbidden for them to have knowledge of the stars, mathematics, physics, philosophy. It was forbidden for them to teach, to read hieroglyphics, to be a scribe. They were only allowed to learn to be hetairai. Know you what an hetaira is? You call them prostitutes, except hetairai were *trained* in the art of making love. Know you that when you are trained to do that, passion dies within the soul; it is no longer there. And since women were not allowed to work, when they were ''old'' and were cast into the streets, they had to whore for their daily bread. It is a great truth.

So men had their way with women, and it was acceptable. (But how different are you *this* day, you who accept so many things?)

Now, men had the soul; they were the chosen lot. They were ''the entities of God,'' and their *duty* was to feed the war machine. They could not weep, because if they wept they would be likened unto a woman, and it was a *hideous* condemnation to be called a woman! So they couldn't cry, nor could they be soft and tender. They had to be hard and ruthless and all things that are indicative of being a man.

So afraid were they, and yet so suppressed in their fear were they, that they fought like mad dogs, a powerful army!

Men were raised to fight one another. When they went into battle they couldn't shake, they couldn't show fear. So afraid were they, and yet so suppressed in their fear were they, that they fought like mad dogs, a *powerful* army! And every head they hacked off meant not having theirs done away with; so they fought with great fervor and zeal. (Remember, all of their emotions were being recorded in their souls.)

Know you what a warrior's prize was when a battle was over? The women and children. That is when rape and pillage began. The men took out all their fears and frustrations through sexual explosion. It was a no thing for a woman to be molested by a legion, because *pain* had also become instrumental in sexual fulfillment.

(Sighs deeply) Women lost their soulmates during the fall of women because men were not allowed to feel. They were disconnected from their soulmates by virtue of belief, dogma, and social acceptance. So now we have, afloat in the sea of human turmoil, men and women who are disconnected from the reality of each other.

What began to occur is that life after life of coming back onto the wheel of incarnation, there was nothing happening between men and women—soulmates—on a soul level. The women were now alone, and they could not understand, because they were without the male aspect of their being with whom could balance their knowledge. Men were isolated from their women and could not understand them on a soul level because they were not allowed to consider them as equals. (In the days that I am speaking of, if you said that this woman or this man was your soulmate, your equal, you would have been put to death, because a woman was *never* allowed to stand equal to a man.)

You want to check all of this out? Go to your libraries and delve deeply into your history and what was practiced—what *is* practiced even this day in your time. There are many religions that still forbid women to worship with men because they are considered "less than." And they must cover their hair, their crowning glory, lest they "tempt the heart of an honest man." Women are *still* endeavoring to be equal with men, even in what is called your sophisticated societies. What is going *on?* How ignorant *are* you?

Have I made you uncomfortable? You *should* be!

Now, the next pattern to evolve was that when many

Have I made you uncomfortable? You should be!

women chose to return, they would "cross over" and choose a male embodiment through which to do so. Why? Because they saw the honor that was bestowed upon men. And they thought that their lives would be much easier if they didn't have to bear children. They thought it would be much easier not to be raped and molested and endure the pain. Also, many men, not wanting to go to battle, wanting to be able to weep like the women or to be taken care of like the women, felt it would be easier if they came back as the female gender. So *they* crossed over. Are you understanding what is happening now? You would have to know that you have lived before to reason this understanding that is an epic truth in your history.

What happens when a female, negative energy, enters into a male energy organism where the seals are designed to respond to positive energy? What happens when a positive energy entity enters into a body where the seals are supposed to respond to negative energy? You have what are called "hybrids." You have *confusion*.

So now you have the woman, who is really a man, being molested at the age of three—and he is being molested by a man! Now you have the "man" going to battle at the age of twelve and swinging a broadsword. The little girl, who is now embodied in a man's energy, evolves into a hybrid form that is rough-hewn like a man but emotionally a woman. The body is definitely male but the soul is female.

Crossovers are hybrids, often lovers of their own kind, a union that produces nothing. And when you have a union of male and female in which one is a crossover, you have negative with negative or positive with positive. When you have that, they *repel* each other; in other words, they move away from each other. Know you that cellular mass cannot *evolve* in a repelling process?

What happens when an entity crosses over but its soulmate holds on? One loses strength while the other gains it. And they have no connection with one another in order to draw from one another. What is the soulmate of a crossover doing? It is *repelling* the other. Not only did these soulmates not have a very good communication to start with, they are now being pushed further away rather than being drawn together *harmoniously*.

What if the priest and the prophet had never come? There would have been no such thing as hybrids or crossovers. And what would your world be like today? There would be no decadence.

You know, you have brothers who live far, far away from here, in other places. And they are of such intelligence that you would say that they are of a "higher" intelligence. No, they are simply virtuous. Vir-tu-ous. They do not molest their children, a common practice in your society. And it is not that one must be physically *doing* it. All you have to do is *think* about it, and it is a reality.

What *are* your fantasies? What buttons are you pushing in your soul of the memory of primeval times that were im-balanced? You are still continuing in the same context. You still molest your children. You look at things that portray the degradation of innocence. It is common to you! You listen to music that is inspired by sexual violence. You say you don't hear the words? You hear *all* of them! The soul is aware of *everything*.

In your beginning on this plane, copulation was an act of passion; it was the height of passion. Passion did not *mean* simply the release of spermatazoa and the muscle contractions of the beloved womb. It was creation! creative power! the creative element. Passion was the Is, the great Thought, con-templating. And the product of passion was light!

Know you what your soul now determines copulation to be? Ug-ly. You call it "sex," and to you it is ugly. It has fallen from grace. Know you why some men can't get an erection without thinking about molesting a child or raping a man in his rectum? Because they have done those things, and the memory of the *violence* of sexual experience is the only button that can create sexual arousal. They have to *make* sex happen.

Men spill their seed, and they think it's natural. It's as natu-ral as dying! Because every moment you do that, you are

You listen to music that is inspired by sexual violence. You say you don't hear the words? You hear all of them! The soul is aware of everything!

spending your life force, and it's dying in front of you on barren ground.

Who are many of you making love to? It isn't your lover, because you are fantasizing about someone else—or some *thing* else! And when you are making love to an entity, how many people are you really sleeping with? Three, not one, because there are *four* of you in bed. *(Audience laughs.)* Remember soulmates?

Men, you degrade your women. You snicker, you laugh at them. You are still de-virtuizing them. You look at pictures of their naked bodies with their private parts exposed. It isn't passion that you are feeling; it's *superiority* that you are feeling. You think that's natural? That is decadence. Have you ever imagined your mother in one of those magazines? And your penises, you wear them like badges! The penis was created to be an extension for placing the seed into the nest so that you could be here this moment. That's what it was created for by divine gods, who saw the penis as a holy, co-creative thing. And yet there are places in your marketplace where they *sell* them, imitations.

You men fantasize about your penises, you compare them, and you think a penis determines manhood. Do you know where that thought is coming from? From your memories of long, long ago that are *still* alive. Oh, you have lived many lifetimes since then, and the stage has changed. Time has changed, technology has changed, but the thoughts are still there. It's a new body but the same old you, because you will not cease pushing the buttons in your soul that keep taking you back to that time.

You are marauders of children. You despise their innocence, their freedom, their virtue. That is decadence. It is a sign of your inward collapse, the collapsing of the divine soul. It is a sign that you are shutting down your brain and becoming lower than survival. You would rather take your gold and spend it on a song that portrays moral decadence than to buy foodstuffs to store for a winter coming quickly on the land. You will take the pence and you will go and watch the motion

It isn't passion that you are feeling; it's superiority that you are feeling.

of pictures that exploit decadence, and yet you call it a grand performance. That should make you weep a *thousand* years. But you are below survival and you are desensitized to virtue.

Had women never fallen from equality, none of what I have told you would ever have existed, and Superconsciousness would have been long established on this plane. Had the fall of women never occurred, you would now have a fully operational brain instead of less than a third. You would not have disease and you would not have old age, because you would be timeless. Did you know that? Your brothers who you would say are of higher intelligence, do you know that they have lived millions of years in the same body? It is a truth.

You who are decadent are falling apart in your souls. When the winter comes you will drop like flies, I assure you. Nature is getting rid of decadence because it goes against the continuum, the virtue, and the purity of Life. It is warring against Life; and it's a war which the natural element of Is will always win, I assure you. That is how it is.

Why do you men feel so *sexual?* Because that's all you think about! Have you ever held on to your seed rather than spilling it? Have you ever tried just *being* and allow natural passion to engage you? Very few of you do. It is all forced, and you have to get more and more violent with your fantasies in order to make it happen. When you do that, you are pushing the buttons and re-enacting a primeval imbalance.

Why are women prone to not having orgasms? Because in their souls, sexual expression has been equated with violence and survival rather than pleasure.

What is happening to the soulmates of those who fantasize violence, who spill their seed, who are molesters of children, who are marauders of sexual expression? They are becoming enlightened to what you are doing and they are not condoning it. They are picking up the truth of the nature of your being and they are repelling you. The more collapsed you are inwardly, the further away your soulmates are.

Nature is warring upon that which despises life. And the war will affect many entities, not only crossovers but those of you who, even in the quietness of your being, live in a state of decadence. There is nothing wrong with living in decadence, understand that, if that is your chosen destiny. But know that you are not in harmony with life in its natural flow; thus you shall perish from this plane, and your kind will become extinct. And who will be left? The meek of the earth. *(Toasts)* To Life! Forever, and ever, and ever. So be it!

Audience: So be it.

Ramtha: Now, Yeshua ben Joseph, Buddha Amin, Ra-Tabin, were each great christs. And each had spoken, "Behold, in the days to come, the meek shall inherit the earth." Ever know what "the meek" meant? *Simple-minded entities.* Everyone always thought that "simple-minded" meant that you were stupid. But know you that it has been through simplicity that your greatest geniuses have come forth? Simplicity.

The meek are the aligned, and the aligned are *open-minded;* they are simple. Rather than worshipping in a temple, they go into a forest and watch nature at sunrise. Or they dance like elfin kings and queens under a starry night. They are simple, and they love who they are enough to be that. That is why they will be left. And it is from such virtue and simplicity that Superconsciousness will be born upon this plane. It is at hand.

If you do not love yourselves enough to become simple entities, you are going to die. That is the way it is. You can make all the excuses you want to, you can blame everyone else for your fate, but it won't change it. And *who* created it? You did! *You* make the difference.

To say "I cannot change" is a cop out!

To say "I cannot change" is an illusion; it is a cop out! You don't *want* to change! Remember "want"? You don't want to give up your boy lovers or girl lovers. You don't want to give up your decadence. So be it. It is all right, and you are still loved. But know that your hour is at hand. Great plagues liken unto those that occurred in the past of your times are coming back; they have are already begun. You are beginning to relive your decadence all over again, yet you are *insensitive* to it, and you just keep pushing those buttons. Well, it's coming to a great pinnacle, and your decadence will soon be over, *never again* to come forward. It will be *old soul business*.

You want to be masters? Don't be afraid to change. Do you understand? And don't tell me that it is not *in you* to change! I *know* better! Because there is a god that lives within you that has power and dominion over *all things* — and you are choking it to death! But it is still there. When you stop pushing the buttons, you allow wisdom to come forth. When you stop pushing the buttons, you allow your soul to own the experience; then the decadence becomes a pearl of wisdom, and you no longer have to live it over and over again.

There is a god that lives within you that has power and dominion over all things—and you are choking it to death!

If you are desiring to be a master, stop accepting thoughts into your mind that push buttons within your soul. Do I have to tell you what these thoughts are? Are you that insensitive that you don't know? *Wake up!* I will send you runners that will push all of your buttons. They are going to be blatant in front of you. So be it.

Now, you women! You love/hate your men. You, master it! Men, you love/hate your women. Master it! If the only place you can find solace and peace and joy is under some grand old being called a tree, then *go there* — for the sake of life. Do you understand? Do you hear? *(The audience sits in stunned silence.)*

Now you "know." Now you are "in knowledge of," you are enlightened *to*. And don't tell me you cannot make a difference. *I* am making a difference! A grand one. Soon I will become a "fashionable entity." Know you what that is? It means everyone will know my name. *(Shrugs)* Big deal. Well, it is not *important* that they know my name; it *is* important that they have heard these words and listened to them. *That* makes a difference. Knowledge engages enlightenment.

All you have to do is cease pushing the buttons; then the soul becomes healed and the light begins to extend. And love? It is indeed there, and it lifts up social consciousness.

Can you say "no" and walk away, and not care what others think? Know you the weed? How many of you can pass up a joint? You say, "It's not very strong. It's the thing to do."

But did you know that you are *killing* your brain? Every moment you get high, do you know what the high is? It is the death of your brain cells, which cannot be replaced because they do not divide and multiply. When your brain is gone, you can no longer receive the essence and the thought of the god that surrounds you; you are dead of mind. Every time you inhale the weed, you are killing yourself; you are losing the ability to be happy because there is less and less there to facilitate the electrum of the thoughts that incur joy.

Many of you can't even say "no" to a joint. You cannot walk away from decadence with your head held up high because you love yourself enough to know that that is not where you belong. You can't even turn off your television sets, because if you did, you would feel that you are alone.

Know you how you can know an entity? Look at what he reads. Look at what he watches. Look at what he hangs upon his walls and puts in his drawers. You don't have to be a psychic. All you have to do is *look*. That will tell you everything about where his soul is and what he is feeding it. So take a look at your walls, your library, and what *you* are watching. That says it all.

Know you that you can make love with the fervor of original passion if you simply leave your body alone and let it talk to you? It's true. Let your soul talk to you; it will tell you when you are ready.

There are many of you whose loins and wombs run your lives. What you look like in your mirror is the next greatest thing that drives you. Well, there will come an hour for every entity when those things have faded away and become no more. It is the hour when the christ has arisen within you. The more you begin to own your power, the more you will find the desire in your first seal dimishing, because you are allowing the power to go upward. Celibacy can never be forced. When you force it you create frustration. Celibacy is a natural reaction to waking up from the dream of social consciousness and becoming a master. It is merely a replacement of power. It is allowing the feeling within your loins to permeate your entire being. Understand?

Audience: Yes.

Ramtha: Now, I have a bargain to make with the lot of you. Know you what is called television—the boxes that create the past over and over again? What do you usually watch? Or rather, what are you entertained by? Your soapy operas. And oh! how soapy they *are,* trauma after trauma, blow upon blow—and no one is ever happy! Well, when I was on my rock, there was no television. I had only the wind, the seasons, starry nights, the moon, and the laughter of children to teach me.

Now, the bargain is not that I desire for you to go sit on a rock. Your rumps could never handle it. And what would your neighbors think? But on your television there are programs that are called "nature." Know you what I speak of? I desire for you, for seven days in your time, to plug it in, turn it on, and watch *nature.* Bargain?

Audience: Bargain.

Ramtha: I desire for you to see what taught me about the Unknown God and myself in relationship to it. And if you are missing out on your soapy operas, I'll tell you how to get caught up. Just do a "reading." You don't even have to do that; they are *very* predictable. *(Toasts)* To nature! and a new understanding. So be it!

Audience: So be it.

Ramtha: There will come an hour when women and men are in harmony once again. That is certain. That is nature.

Now, I desire to speak to you in regard to judgment. How does one abstain from decadence without judging those who participate in it? By *allowing* everyone to have their truth and loving them *in freedom.*

God, the Is, that which is termed Life, is in a state of forever allowing, correct? Well, if it wasn't, life could not go on. So, God *allows.* And God is neither good nor bad; it *is.* Nor is God perfection, because perfection is a limitation; it limits the process of going onward into forever. God is the ongoing Isness that simply is, and it allows every thing, which it is, to be. The Is, that allows you, loves you in freedom for the *wild* expression of itself.

So what about all of those entities who are dying of the plagues [AIDS] and the war of nature that is becoming more and more? Well, there are those in religion who proclaim they are spokespersons for God; and they say, in the name of God, that these entities are being punished, that they are condemned.

Religion cannot exist without good and evil. And there is more effort spent on punishing and highlighting evil than there is on seeking *wisdom*. But I will tell you a great truth that is in harmonious flow with what I have taught you: These entities who are dying from the plagues are neither good nor bad; they are simply expressing, and they are learning from that experience. It is something they wanted. They chose it and they got it. Is it not enough to know that they have taken life to its lowest form and that life is now rebuking them? Is it not enough that these entities are dying a most painful, humiliating, and certain death without your sitting in judgment of them? Is that not *enough?*

These entities are God! And they will live again, in another place, another time. They are not going anywhere to be tormented. Losing life is torment enough.

If the morning to come was your last morning, would you sleep in? Good question?

Let me ask you this: If the morning to come was your last morning, would you sleep in? Good question? What would you be doing? You would be living *every moment*. And while dawn was not so grand before, you would see it like you never saw it before. What did it take for you to appreciate its splendor? Knowing you would never see it again.

Isn't it an irony that it takes disease and death to make you aware of life, the grandest gift of all. *Why* do you wait for your *last* moments to appreciate it?

These entities are counting down their mornings. The reason the disease is slow is that it allows them the painful review of their lives and the opportunity to come to peace and terms with that which is within them.

Love them. They are your brothers. Love them! Loving

them doesn't mean you have to go and wipe the vileness from their sores. It means *respecting* them. It means allowing them to be, without judgment. Their own judgment is upon them, just like it is upon you in *your* wildest fantasies because you are going to *become* your fantasies. Allow them without judging them. They are hard-pressed to see tomorrow's daybreak while *you* sleep in.

I ponder the darkness in the minds and souls of mankind, darkness so grave that there is barely any light to cast a shadow of hope, an emotion that purports to be built on the love of God. These entities who say they love God and speak for him, prove it in very dark ways, for they are busy casting their neighbors into hell-fire because their neighbors don't believe the same way they believe. They are so narrow-minded in their polarity that there is no room for Is.

(Clears his throat and drinks) No wonder so many entities do not know or love God, for those who say they represent God propose fearsome threats to their lives.

(Clears his throat again) Know you what this seal is? *(Points to his throat)* It is called the fifth seal of expression. When use I this body and I am giving you a truth that is great in emotion, this seal begins to shut down. It is an old term called being "choked up." So, oftentimes I get choked up in this body.

Love God, Life, with all of your might and all of your beauty. Love all for their unique truths. Be a light to yourself. Judge *no* man. Allow all to be. And take joy in your children and don't make them grow up so fast.

Because I speak out in regard to dogma, I am condemned as an evil entity. (Of course! To them *everything* is evil.) But I *love* those who are ensnared in their dogmas.

The cure for decadence is breaking away, ceasing the buttons, loving yourself, and removing the judgments. Life is going to take care of and eliminate that which is not in harmony with it. Have compassion and be allowing in the process. Understand?

Audience: Yes.

No wonder so many entities do not know or love God, for those who say they represent God propose fearsome threats to their lives.

Ramtha: Now, your rectums were not made for intercourse. Your seed was not created to be spilled into napkins or linen. As long as you hold on to it, it is *power*. Your breasts were not created to proclaim you are a woman. They were created to suckle children into life.

You women, if you sleep around you are going to die, because the epidemic will reach you inevitably. Men, if you count your "scores," you are going to die because you are giving your power away to an illusion.

Reclaim your virtue. Have honor in your seed and in your womb. If you don't want to experience violence, don't fantasize it, don't watch it, don't read it. That is walking away. And that is loving yourself.

If you don't want to experience violence, don't fantasize it, don't watch it, don't read it. That is walking away. And that is loving yourself.

Did you know that it takes a polarity to have war? There is no war if one accuses you of being wrong and you *allow* them their accusation, because there is no re-action. Walk away and allow. That is being a master.

Am I a moralist? I am God! I am not "moral." That would mean I am "immoral." I am neither. I am!

It is all right to look back on your path and see it as "all right," for that allows it to become wisdom. But it is the hour to go *forward* in waking up. When you wake up, your soulmates wake up. When you hold on to your virtue, they reclaim theirs. It's a natural reaction. And when you have cleaned yourselves up, you will be ready to see a grand, grand divine event. Understand?

Audience: Yes.

Ramtha: If you are wanting your soulmate because you are wanting them to bring you your happiness, it won't happen; because that, *again,* is seeking something outside of yourself to make life better. The soulmate epilogue is a natural re-action to finding god within and living a noble and virtuous life that every morning means something. And perhaps one day you will meet that magnificent plant that wraps itself around itself and collects the dew that makes the pool. And if you stay long enough you may even see the little frog emerge from the pool. What a wondrous thing that would be to experience. What intelligence!

This audience has been an endeavor, through language, to make you aware of a feeling. If the feeling is happening inside your souls, rejoice. Rejoice! For then you are claiming the unspeakable truth. If speaking to you *evenly* has brought about the surrender where you begin to really look at yourselves, it has all been worth it, hasn't it? And when you own all of your emotions, you will live to see many daybreaks, a new time, a new consciousness, a grand experience that is worth being alive for.

Now, I have stepped on many toes, but they *needed* it.

(Looks at the somber faces in the audience) You know, it is *all* an illusion! Because you can change your mind *in a moment* and the *whole* drama changes. Did you know that? You can close your eyes and block out the sun. You can plug up your nose and miss the smell of a grand rose. See how *powerful* you are? It doesn't take a bunch of miracles to prove that! All you have to do is *want*. There is no one who can do that *for* you. It's up to you to desire it. If you're not strong enough and you are wanting help, I'm here. If you have to hear this message and this teaching a *thousand times* until you own it, do it! Because every moment you do, little by little I am chipping away at your stubbornness. If you come back to this audience it does not mean you're a follower. (You can't even go where I go! If you could, you wouldn't be here, that is for certain.) It means you want to know. And whatever you have to do, however *far* you must travel, however many times you must come back, do it! Do you understand?

Audience: Yes.

Ramtha: You know, when the game of warring was over for me, my army wanted to continue going on. Know you what is it like to stand alone against two and one-half million people? But I did not get up from my rock when the whole of my army was talking behind my back at safe distances. For seven years I sat there. And all the while, they called me weak, spineless. They spat on me in secret. Even the children would run around mocking me. *My* army did that to *me*—after *all* I did for them! *(Audience laughs uproariously.)* Well, that is all right. I understand what it is like to live in social consciousness; I had my own. I *created* the way they thought! *I* was the barbarian—they went along for the ride.

Whether it takes you seven years or one hundred years of allowing, there will come one fine moment when you'll get it; everything will turn on. Know you the term "the lights are turning on"? They *will,* but it will be from a *natural* evolution; the knowingness will evolve naturally. Little by little you'll grow. You will find yourself picking up the pieces. You will find yourself owning yourself, more and more, and that the need for someone else to make you happy is becoming less and less. Little by little you will realize that you are it. *You are it!* You are evolving to a *whole*, and you are becoming the light. The more you own, the more powerful you become—but not over *others*. If you use your power for that, I will bring you down. Understand?

Audience: Yes.

Ramtha: This has certainly been a different intensive. I have taught you things this day that I have not taught you before because now you are ready, you have grown. And it has not been from what you heard this day as much as it has been from what you felt, because *feeling* is the great teacher; it is you teaching you.

(Walks over to the "old pro" section) You, this wondrous little group, you are being polished. Since last we met, you have had many thoughts, many emotions, many questions. And there have been those of you who have rebuked me. That is all right; I still love you. You rebuke me because it takes the pressure off you. But you should not do this because you are being *pressured* to. This should be a "want." You can always stop any moment you *want* to. You can always put the brakes on and remain stuck in time and stuck in decadence, which you have been. But if you *want* to hold on to these teachings you'll go right into forever with what you are learning.

I *love* you. I *bless* you. It takes a great entity to come to this audience, because those who come here are ready to face

It takes a great entity to come to this audience, because those who come here are ready to face themselves.

themselves. I am going to send you a host of runners who are bearers of joy. They are tributes to something splendid. Success, you will have it like you never had it before. Brilliance will be there, so much so that you will think that everyone possesses it because it was so easy for you to have. Those of you who have been waiting to catch the drops of knowingness and do something with them, you are going to have *all* you ever wanted. All of it! That is the blessing for one who perseveres.

Why do you come back to my audiences? Because you are a sadist? *(Audience laughs.)* You come back here because the god within you *knows* it has been living in a dream—because why would you want to live if life was *only* the continuum of pain and agony? The god in you knows that there is more than this dream, and that all you have to do is wake up and peel away your limitations. What of the cost? If you owned all the gold in universe, and that was the price for these teachings, pay it! It is far greater to own the knowledge of how to make it.

The runners I am sending you are expressions of yourselves, because you cannot go into unlimited existence without knowing yourself.

What is on the other side? A wild adventure that is virgin, that is like the moment when soulmates, wholly pure and virtuous, first looked upon one another. Beyond social consciousness lies such a consciousness. It is virgin; it is pure. It is highly evolved. It is moving forward. My runners come from that place. You are ready to make an advancement, a move, and so they come.

There is joy beyond limitation. How do you get there? I am the teacher of "how to." Once you arrive you are on your own, and that is a wondrous thing.

Know you what backsliding is? If you cop out on yourselves you will backslide into what you are coming out of, one hundredfold. If you go forward you will pass the point of no return. That is where *I* went. Get it?

There are those of you who haven't gotten it yet. That is all

If you go forward you will pass the point of no return. That is where I went.

88

*I am not pitting you
in a race against
one another;
you do that yourselves.*

right. There is no time marker involved here. I am not pitting you in a race against one another; you do that yourselves. This is a movement of individual evolution. Individual! It is most unfair and judgmental to compare yourselves to others who seemingly have got it all together. How do you *know* that they do? You are *not* them. There is no comparison to you. There is not another "you" in same gender. So all you know is where *you* are. *Your* progress is based on *your* wants. Understand?

There are still a few of you who are bent on thinking, "Nothing works for me." So be it. It never *will*. And that is all right. Be unhappy; that is your choice. You are in control.

I love you. Remember me when you are feeling *wonderful*. *(Surveys the audience)* Are you tired?

Audience: No!

Ramtha: I had to *drag* answers out of you earlier! Have you learned?

Audience: Yes.

Ramtha: Have you indeed *felt*?

Audience: Yes.

Ramtha: Are you going to be, allow, love in freedom?

Audience: Yes!

Ramtha: (Smiling) Ah! I love entities of conviction.

Now, you are in a time that is called an "evolution eclipse." Nature is making an about-face yet going forward. Time is moving very quickly. *I* am moving quickly! Know you what a march is? It is when an army of people is on the move. The falling of their footsteps and the beating of the hooves of their steeds quake the earth and send saffron dust whirling into the air giving the illusion of gold. There are those entities who quicken to join the march. And yet there are others who only watch. And before they have wholly comprehended every face that just marched by them, all that remains of the great army is the settling of the saffron dust and the sounds of a distant drummer, somewhere over the hill, far, far away.

The "new age" is already here. It is the age of *consumption* of knowledge—not the pursuit of, but the *allowing* of. And in that age there is no room for limited beliefs. If you come to my audience I will teach you, but *you* are the god. If you are bent on keeping your closed minds, your prejudices, your judgments, your not loving or allowing, I will leave you behind.

I love you. Say what you will in regard to that which I am, but spell my name right. *(Audience laughs.)* There is only one Ramtha, and whatever you perceive me to be does not matter. For whatsoever you see in me, so you are, for everything is a reality only from *your* point of perception.

You have come to this audience to see an *outrageous* entity that no one can explain. For you to come here was the first stretching of your limited minds. For you to *pay* to come here stretched you a lot further! *(Audience cheers and applauds.)* It is a *great* truth. So already you have begun to become unlimited, just by coming here. Those who take these teachings to heart will end up in grand ways, I assure you, for it means letting go, it means changing, it means going forward.

I do not want you to worship me, ever! If I did, I would show you what I am, and, I assure you, I would intimidate you. But all I am now is a little body, a woman's body with a man's essence. When you have evolved and you have owned all that I owned, and you have become a sovereign god, then you will see and know who be I.

I am the Ram, a grand mirror. When you leave this audience I desire for you to worship yourself and God that is within you. And where go you to do that? Where is your temple? Right within you. The purest temple of God, 'tis you.

In the tomorrow of your time I will give you further knowledge on the spiritual science of soulmates. Remember: Do not make a dogma from this science. Do not use it to entice others to be your soulmate. It is unfair to do that to yourselves. Do not utilize this teaching, hang on to it, or have it become your religion. There are many of you who have wondrous mates to your beings. Unless you are bored, hang in there. Because if you go *looking* for your soulmates, you are in for madness. Understand?

If you go looking for your soulmate, you are in for madness.

*Speak to the
lord-god of your being
and hear
what it has to say
back to you.*

Audience: Yes.

Ramtha: That is all for this day; you have had enough. The "enough" has been "heavy furniture." *(Audience laughs in agreement.)* Go and contemplate what you felt this day. Speak to the lord-god of your being and hear what it has to say back to you. And rest this night in your time. Rest! Know you what that means? It means it is not necessary to be "party hearty." To absorb this intensive, you need to rest your bodies. Feed them, bathe them, rest them, and just be. With your dreams will come a restlessness, and yet it will be a peaceful night, for this knowingness is coming into your soul from the god around you and within you; it will penetrate all levels of your consciousness. So you are going to continue to learn even in your state of rest.

When the hour rings out into the valley, and the toll of the bells equates the number called nine, I will meet you again. So be it. *(Audience cheers and applauds.)*

You are worth it all! I love you. Go and be happy. Indeed? So be it.

***

Sunday Morning Session
January 12, 1986

Once members of the audience have taken their seats, Ramtha looks them over warmly, steps down from the platform and begins to mingle with them. He slowly works his way through the audience, stopping to speak to individuals.

Ramtha: *(After carefully stepping through the crowd seated on the floor in front of the stage)* So, you are floor sitters. That is good. Though the carpet is not Persian, 'tis "even ground." If you get a little closer, you seemingly get a better look, eh? And if you get a better look, you think you get a better understanding. Well, try getting close to the wind.

(Walks a few steps and then stops in front of a woman) You are trying to hide your beautiful face? I cannot see it so well. Lady, you don't know how beautiful you really are, but I assure you, you are going to.

(Turns to a man) Scribe, know you how to write down a feeling? I shall see that you know.

(Walks over to a man, looks deeply into his eyes for a moment, goes to the stage, where he pulls a flower from a vase, then returns to present it to the man) Once, you gave my daughter a flower. Now I give you this one. When the color begins to fade, take it and put it in a safe place. It is a treasure beyond treasure. When you are feeling alone, take it out and look at it. It will remind you of your outrageous Ramtha.

(The man tries to express his gratitude.) Words can never captivate emotion; they struggle to express it. You, master,

You don't know how beautiful you really are, but I assure you, you are going to.

are the words called "living emotion."

(Walks over to an older woman and admires her silver hair)
There are those, lady, who hide such beautiful strands of silver mirth. I am pleased that there are still those who wear it in grand glory.

Woman: Thank you.

Ramtha: And notice how well white goes with everything.

(Walks over to a woman on the verge of tears) What can one possibly dream up, lady, that would cause one to be so unhappy? *(Kisses her hands and holds them to his chest)* Know you that joy is but an awakening away? I will show you. So be it.

(Turns to a man) You are listening to the teaching?

Man: Yes.

Ramtha: Feel you the teaching?

Man: Yes.

Ramtha: Understand you what say I?

Man: Most of it, yes.

Ramtha: That is an honorable answer. That which be I is not from outer space; I am from inner space. That which is the All-in-All, entity, does not give hope to humanity unless it is inner. Knowledge is often painful, and yet from pain emerges life. When you acknowledge who and what you are, you can break through the barriers that hold you—not with madness, but with grace. You have learned a lot, master, and you are worth it.

(Slowly walks to back of the hall and stops in front of a woman) You are learning, lady. You have been plunged into fire, you have been pitted against reality and illusion, you have been pitted against practical and impractical, and you have come out like steel. I love you, master, for you are steadfast. There is coming an hour when you will do a great work from all that you have learned here. There are those who wear long robes and proclaim God in the marketplace but feel it not within their souls. But from you, all that is within you shines forth. That is the true message, the grandest teaching. *(Kisses her hands)* I love you.

(Walks past several individuals, acknowledges them, then stops in front of a young woman in a beautiful dress) Silk! Very enchanting. 'Tis beautiful! *(Kisses her hands)* I see that which is the nature nymph, who has been afraid of life, coming forth into the bloom of a woman. 'Tis the last grand experience. Indeed!

(Walks over to an old woman) Little girl! You are liken unto that which is termed an elf. *(Kisses her hands)* There will come an hour when you will gaze into a mirror, and behold! the image will change. In what is liken unto a light that is pearl in its essence and shimmer, you will see a tender maiden gliding across a meadow of honeysuckle and bluebell. And the wind will take her garment of linen and swirl it around her tender body, ever so wispily. And you will see that her face is liken unto a peach, with the blush upon it ripe in its age and beauty. And there, set within the peach, you will see two wondrous gems of color that no color can match. 'Tis the eyes of a maiden, wild and free and innocent. And behold! you will look upon the woman in great wonderment. When the image fades, there will come back the face and, indeed, the age. But ah! those wonderful gems! They are the same beautiful and elusive color.

And you will say, "'Tis been a grand experience."

Woman: Thank you.

Ramtha: Be happy that you are beyond the reach of outrageous youth.

(Returns to the stage and begins his address) I salute you from the lord-god of my being. That which you are, love I greatly.

If your world could conceive of a mass of humanity, regardless of the masks they wear, peacefully cohabitating in a place called paradise, a paradise of breathtaking mornings and captivating nights, those such as you would be the inhabitants. You are a tribute to your people and, indeed, to the human drama. Be exceedingly glad. You've allowed yourself to be uplifted beyond the mundane. And what you have felt in this wondrous, august body, is felt by the *whole* of the world.

What you have felt in this august body, is felt by the whole of the world.

Look upon yourselves. You are wondrous entities, and you are worth the message. You are only beginning to contemplate the glory of what you are. I see it; you are just beginning to feel it. If the world could be as you, what a wonderful place it would be. Indeed?

Audience: Indeed.

Ramtha: (Picks up his glass and toasts with the audience) To that which *allows* life. To Life! Forever, and ever, and ever! So be it!

Audience: So be it!

Ramtha: You are broadening your horizons. You are coming into great knowledge. Indeed, you are on the doorstep of becoming.

Now, I have spoken to you in regard to cleaning up your act—because you *need* to. Why is that important? Not to find your soulmates, but to *live*. To live! Life was not intended to be running amuck, searching for your soulmate. If that was the intent, why would your great god lower and split itself in the first place? You lowered yourself to experience this kingdom because *this* was the *epic* kingdom, the far reaches of Thought manifested, an adventure into self-expression. You lowered yourself because you desired to smell the rose, to lie in a meadow, to plunge your hands into clear water, to put your hands into earth and till it, to pluck a root from the ground and taste it, to feel a midnight breeze, to know what it is to feel warmth.

Life was not intended to be running amuck, searching for your soulmate.

When you created everything here, it was like painting a picture of a wondrous scene, painting it so clearly that the dew drops took on life. And yet, when you endeavored to touch the dew drops that you painted, your hand touched only canvas.

There are many artisans who would love to live where they paint; they would love to *be* what they paint. The painting is only a mirror of the desire. Well, your creation was like a painting. It was like creating a masterpiece but not *being* the masterpiece. So your god split to become the polarization of energized life in order to *become* the texture of the canvas, to *be* the color and the hue.

Soulmates embarked on the enigma called life for the purpose of expression, for the purpose of experiencing unbridled sensation. Their journey into the three-dimensional plane was not for the purpose of *finding* each other because they already *were* each other. Their desire and their lust was to experience and be a part of the painting. When they went on their separate journeys, they *knew* they were always together in a harmonious balance of positive/negative electrum energy, sharing and feeling the *same* soul-source, the same spiritual-electrum force. The soul innately *knows* that it shares with the other. The soul knows; it knows itself.

Know you why you are wanting your soulmate? Because you have forgotten *why* you are here! You have closed down your awareness of what reality truly is and what is truly important. What is *important* is to live!

But when you become blind to the colors of a hummingbird—

When you must be so clean that you no longer put your fingers into the earth—

When you become so busy that you can't arise before daybreak to see the ongoingness of the sunrise, or take the time to become intoxicated with the aroma of honeysuckles in the evening—

When you can't do these things any longer, and *all* you want to do is get out of the painting—*then* you are wanting a soulmate, someone to make you happy, to complete your life. But it will never be complete, masters, until you experience and embrace life, all of it! When you are engaged in the ongoingness of life rather than the petty illusions that you create, you are evolving naturally and are going forward into forever. But you, in your boxes and in your insecure worlds that you've made so neat and tidy, have separated yourselves from life and have created emotional voids; so you search for someone to fill the void. It is your insecurity rather than your love of self that drives you. But only when you love yourself, *wholly,* are you whole and complete. Did you know that?

It is your insecurity rather than your love of self that drives you.

Your purpose for being here is simply to live, because without living, you cannot create your purpose and your destiny in each moment of life. Make sense?

Audience: Yes.

Ramtha: Now, there was an entity who asked me where his soulmate was, and I said, "Vermont" (wherever that is). So he ran amuck, searching high and low for her, spending every pence he had, not leaving *one* body unturned. I watched him scurrying about and I had a jolly good laugh. He soon returned, and he said, "Oh, master, I did not find my soulmate. Perhaps you could give me a specific address."

"What be an address?"

"Well, where someone gets correspondence."

"Ah! correspondence. You mean where runners are sent."

"Indeed."

So I plucked out a number and gave it to him. *(Audience and Ramtha laugh.)* I told you that I was not above or below doing *anything* to get a point across!

Now, along the way, he picked up a lot of lovers. You know, a roll in the hay and all. And he was convinced, *prior* to copulation, that each one was "The One." Isn't it wonderful how after the energy of your first seal is spent, the blush comes off the rose.

You see, he missed the whole teaching: He *is* his soulmate! He is with her continuously! So if he goes to Vermont, *of course* his soulmate is there!

Finally, when he had run out of money and sold everything, he came back and said, "Ramtha, it must be something I'm doing."

"Indeed it is. It is *everything* you are doing."

"But Ramtha, I shan't ever feel complete without this entity."

"Then, master, that is your destiny. Leave my audience."

So he did that. And he cursed me at safe distances. But know you what? He is here in this audience this day.

Man: Yeah! *(Audience laughs.)*

Life should not be a seeking process; it is an allowing gift.

Ramtha: The point is, life should not be a seeking process; it is an allowing gift. To run around looking for someone to plug up your holes, looking for someone to make your day brighter, just isn't going to cut it. If you can't watch the morning sun or dance under the stars like an elf *by yourself,* someone else isn't going to make it any better. Are you getting it?

Soulmates never plotted and planned to get together again because they *knew* they were always together. They knew they were expressing, experiencing, creating, and sharing with one another. That truth and that knowledge was known for two and one-half million years after the gods' advent onto this plane. It was forgotten with the "fall of women."

Though many of you came here desperately seeking to find your soulmates, know you that seeking is an enslavement and a limitation? *Allowing* a soulmate is unlimited life. Get it? How it works is, once you *know* that there is such a creature lurking somewhere (maybe Vermont, perhaps the moon) and you start peeling away the limitations that you have racked up over lifetimes, the soul begins to talk to you, emotionally; that is how it speaks. The knowledge I am giving you begins the process of peeling away so that you can begin to *live,* for living is the grand gift. Once you start removing every limitation that you have imposed upon yourself, little by little you reclaim your power and you draw closer to the mate of your being. Understand?

Audience: Yes.

Ramtha: Now, reclaiming your power. It is all right to ask the advice of others, as long as you realize that is *their* truth. If it helps you make a decision, so be it. But try asking yourself *first.* You are not in the habit of doing that because you are used to living by everyone else's directives. Try asking yourself for the answer and then allow your soul to speak to you.

You women, it is all right to paint your faces. That is beautiful, and you are all artists. And your perfumes, though you bought them somewhere and they belonged to some other creatures, it is all right to wear them. But *who* are you wearing them for? Are you smelling good for *you* or for someone else? Are you losing weight because someone wants you to? If you look into a reflector and like what you see, why are you want-

If you can't watch the morning sun or dance under the stars by yourself, someone else isn't going to make it any better.

ing to change it? Who created the ideal anyway? Don't you know that if a famine hits your land, the ones who are thin, thin, thin, are going to die first? They shan't weather a fortnight. Don't you know what fat is? It's the storing up of all the extra goodies that you really didn't need, so that when a famine does hit, or you have to run for your life, you've got a store on hand to draw from. Your body desires to prepare for winter, but you are wanting one long summer!

Getting you to ask *you,* getting you to love *you,* is all that matters because *that* is who you must live with and feel with. When you begin to do that, you are becoming free. Free! That allows you to begin to break out of your little box and to stretch your imagination and your thoughts. Imagine not having to worry about how you appear to others or what they think about you. If that is off your mind and you are free of it, know how you can live? Happily. Happily! Because you will do only those things that bring you joy. And every moment you are doing that, you are sharing it with your other self; it uplifts the entity.

This knowledge I have given you cleans you up to receive a new understanding—that you don't have to own, have, or be with your soulmate to be complete. Do you understand?

You don't have to own, have, or be with your soulmate to be complete. Do you understand?

Audience: Yes.

Ramtha: Now, I have taught my audiences that one must ascend with his soulmate. That is a truth. But any moment you ascend, even alone, 'tis with the mate of your being. For the eternal Is is without time, distance or space. There is *no* separation. Everything is *now.*

You are, simply, already you. You are a whole entity. So why do you still need all of the runners to come? For the arduous task of unfolding you into this understanding. For the arduous task of unmasking and removing all of your fears and judgments so that this simple understanding can get through. Once the runners come and the knowledge begins to be understood, then you will begin to see the becoming of unlimited self.

Those of you who are still bent on finding this poor,

wretched creature, know that you'll die empty-handed.

Now, completion. You are a part of another "you" whose destiny is the grand adventure called life—to explore it, learn, and gain from it. Your souls and spirits share. You move in and out of experiences together. What you are feeling this moment, the other is feeling. What you are seeing this day in understanding and revelation, the other is seeing in psychic visions, *deja vu*. Know you *deja vu?* It is when you have never been to a place before and yet you've had a vision of it. If you visit the pyramids and you feel like you've been there before, the likelihood is that you lived there in a past life. But let's say you had never seen this building in *this* lifetime, and yet you had a vision of it five years ago. So you come here, and here it is. *Who* was seeing it five years ago? Your *soulmate* was here five years ago. Are you getting it? It's how you share energy. You are connected through your seals, your soul (which runs your seals), and the god of your beings that holds you both together; 'tis the same god.

Knowledge of this simple science allows you to be free of insecurity. Know what that is? The feeling that you've got to *have* someone to show the world that you *are* someone; the feeling that it's a crime to be alone.

When you become aware of your mate, you can do wonderful things. You can send them a feeling, intentionally. Sort of like: "Dear John, sorry I could not make it this evening. I love you, anyway. Stay in touch." (I read that from an entity's script only three days ago.) You can talk to your mate by *feeling*, asking the entity to share a knowingness with you. The entity will pick up that feeling and will be propelled, perhaps, to go to a certain place because the feeling is drawing him there. Have you ever felt a draw to do something? It's often because your mate is wanting to know something. And so you go, experience, and you say, "Now I know. Big deal." But your mate is saying, "Wonderful! I *feel* it! And if I feel it, I own the wisdom of it!"

When you learn to use this science, what happens is, you and your mate begin to draw each other together; you are coming together to center at the point called "being." To come to a state of is, of being, is the absolute acceptance of total god with total self.

The more you become aware of your other self, the closer in expression the two of you become because you are "crossing over" energy experiences. The woman will draw her soulmate unto her and she will venture into his soul, still possessing the entirety of who she is, and she will experience the characteristic of the man that she needs in order to feel complete. She will go into his soul and spirit and draw the emotion from his experiences recorded in his soul.

You may see a very passive woman who is very compassionate but not strong. At any moment, she can feel her soulmate, draw on his soul experience, and gain strength. The woman is still a woman, still compassionate, but now strong, more assertive and more balanced. Get it?

The man who doesn't know how to cry, who lives in locked emotion, who is angry, who is hurt and doesn't know how to release his emotions—when he understands this science, he can draw closer to his other self, the female of his being, and he can pass into her soul, carrying all that he is with him. He can pass into her spirit and soul, and he can begin to weep like a babe and cry, perhaps, a *thousand* tears. Those tears will be to make up for seven and one-half million years of suppressed fear, anger, hurt, and confusion that were never allowed to be expressed, except *sexually.*

So he passes into the woman and he finds the tender parts, the allowing, the tears, the *forbidden* tears! He feels her soul and spirit, which *is* a vital part of himself, and then he returns unto his own perimeter, released. His soul has poured out its locked emotions because it was allowed to. All that he has denied for seven and one-half million years, he can now say that he owns. He returns as a strong man yet one who is also tender, soft, and without violence, who can weep at a sunrise because he is endowed with feelings, with understanding.

There are many men who are this way, who have been accused of being crossovers. They are *not* crossovers; they are *aligned*. When they cease listening to the pettiness of social consciousness and love who they are, they will realize that they are complete. Complete.

The science of soulmates is an unspeakable truth, an adventure into the sharing of feelings with someone else who is really you. The more you know in feelings, the more your soulmate knows because you "pass through" the knowledge. This "passing through," this alignment process, can occur in this room; it can occur regardless of where the mate of your being is because it is occurring in knowingness. You receive the feelings of it and you know it. Do you understand?

Audience: Yes.

Ramtha: Now, soulmates often lose the desire for copulation with their opposites because they have completed the experience of copulation, sexual experience. Thus they allow the power to move from the first seal and make its trek through all of the seals in an upward flow. The man's desire to lie with women is not there, yet love is there. The woman's desire to lie with men is no longer there, yet she loves them.

Mastery of the sexual experience allows the completion of the human drama and permits you, through the opening of all your seals, to become a christ. You cannot become a christ if you are riddled with sexual prejudice and hang-ups. When you stop living only in your loins and start living in the spirit, the totality of yourself, the god of yourself, your judgments of men and women will cease, your love will be equal for all of them, and your joy will become greater and greater. You cannot become a christ until you accept and own both the yin and the yang, the positive and negative of your being, man and woman. When you love and own and accept all that God is, then you are complete; then you own the power of an awakening christ; you are a master who is born, who walks the earth, who is endowed with the kingdom of heaven.

Now, there are *very, very* few soulmates who ever meet each other in the physical. They are rare, rare, rare! If they do meet before they have mastered their hang-ups, the union is *explosive*, because each is confronting all of his pettinesses at

The science of soulmates is an unspeakable truth, an adventure into the sharing of feelings with someone else who is really you.

102

once. It is like wrestling with yourself. And how many times have you made yourself miserable, unhappy? Well, multiply that then.

Now you know that it is very unlikely that your husband, your wife, or your lover is your soulmate. You can *say* they are. If that makes you feel better, go for it. That is all right. But *you* are the mate of your being. Your soulmate is expressing in another gender, but it is *in you*. The eyes of your soulmate are the eyes of *yourself*. You understand?

Audience: Yes.

Ramtha: (Looks compassionately at audience) A lot of weeping women.

(Sweeps his glass off the table and toasts them) To fewer broken hearts!

Audience: (Starting to laugh) To fewer broken hearts!

Ramtha: (Laughing with them) I love you, you motley crew!

Now, remember the path of joy? It's *your* path. It is up to *you* to make yourself happy, because you are the recipient of only the joy that *you* have induced. So, wanting to be locked up with someone else is a limitation if it doesn't bring you joy. If you are married, and the entity you are sharing with brings you joy, stick with it, because joy is the path that leads you to the understanding of soulmates and unlocks the door of christus.

Wonderful knowledge you have been given these days, knowledge that has never been taught on this plane. There are some of you who will dismiss it. That is all right. But there will come an hour when you will seek to remember everything that was spoken here because it will have become *vital*.

(Addressing the "old pros") I want to ask you over here a question, and I want you to think about it. If you look at someone and your vision has two options: to see them as disgusting or to see them as god; and if there is a reward for each vision, with the reward for seeing them as disgusting being that *you* become disgusting, and the prize for seeing them as God being that you become God, *which would you choose?*

Wanting to be locked up with someone else is a limitation if it doesn't bring you joy.

Every moment you see someone as other than "is" you have judged *yourself,* you have lessened yourself. *Who* is worth losing *you* over? Have you ever thought of it that way? Who is *worth* that? Every moment you make it a point to see someone's shortcomings and hotly elaborate on them, you are losing yourself, you are losing your power, because whatever you see in others is the perception of yourself. They are only a mirror that reflects you.

If I was my old self again, and you were my enemy, it would be a breeze to bring you down because your tongues wag in forked ways. But know that when you do that, you are only ensnaring your own selves. Do you *hear* me?

Old Pros: Yes!

Ramtha: Do you remember that I said I would send your judgments back to you one hundredfold? Well, hold on! You are going to get all of your judgments back. Enjoy them all!

Now, this does not mean I don't love you. I do and always will. One day you will truly realize that you are worth it. It is sort of wonderful, if you think about it, that one such as I would come to the likes of you and make a big deal out of your lives. Well, you *are* worth it—when you wake up. Asleep, you are dead weight, *heavy* furniture. But that is all right; there are coming grander days in which you will wake up from the dream. Bless the runners as they come. Love the reflections that you see; they help polish the light. If someone slaps you on your cheek, tell them to hit harder on the other one. *Whatever* it takes for you to wake you up, *let it happen!*

Whatever it takes for you to wake you up, let it happen!

I am a staunch teacher, to be certain. But I love you like no one else loves you. When you wake up, then *you* take over. Understand? So be it.

Old Pros: So be it.

Ramtha: (Walks back over to the newcomers and addresses them) Aren't you glad that you aren't part of the graduate class? There *is* something to be said for ignorance!

(Addressing entire audience) You are ripe, ripe. Knowledge brings many gifts. You are ripe to receive them all.

Now, what of you entities who are still bent on being unhappy? It's *your* problem, and you *can* change it—if you *want* to. You are equipped to get what you want out of this life. Anything you want you can manifest by desiring it from the lord-god of your being and then allowing it to happen. Allowing it. Know you what "allow" means? You don't sit and say, "It should have been here by 3:30!" The manifestation will never come when you put a time to it, because time is an illusion. Just know and allow.

Now, I wish to give you a grand teaching about manifestations, particularly those concerning material values.

Have you ever wanted something so much but found that when you got it, it wasn't such a big deal? The reason that material things are created in the first place is to give you a feeling experience from them. What happened through your wanting and dreaming and fantasizing about it is that you created the reality of that feeling *right within you*. So, when you got it, it was no longer as fulfilling as you thought it would be—because you *already* received the feeling that you were wanting to experience.

You all have the power to manifest every desire you have.

A master overcomes every limitation he has by owning up to them—by accepting the thought, embracing the feeling of it, and living through the emotion. Then he owns it; he owns the wisdom. Once he owns all his limitations, there are no longer any buttons in his life that keep bringing him back into a limited consciousness. Soon, he reaches the door of no return because he has become impeccably happy. Once he has become that and is "in full knowledge of," he can never return to the murk and mire of social consciousness. Why? It doesn't *exist* any longer.

When you call forth a desire from the lord-god of your being, you become immersed in the *feeling* of your desire, which is what allows the manifestation to occur. Until you realize that you can own the feeling from the desire without having to experience it in matter, you will receive all the things you ever wanted.

You all have the power to manifest every desire you have. You are heavily endowed with that power. It is also innate to your being to know the answer to every question you ask. All you have to do is ask *you*. The knowledge that will come will allow you wake up and get in tune, if you will, to greater thoughts; that is what opens up your brain more and more.

Ask yourself, the god within you, and it will send you the runners. It will manifest whatever is necessary to give you the answer *emotionally*. The more you ask yourself, the greater the vibrant god within you becomes.

Now, you've heard of the ''second coming of Christ'' that has been prophesied. Well, it is a *true* prophesy. But it is not the return of Yeshua ben Joseph [Jesus Christ]. The return of christ is when the christ is realized in *all peoples*. It is the power within you waking up. The knowledge that I have taught you these days is the knowledge of the christ. It is the understanding that opens, that allows, that wakes you up.

There is a great battle that occurs before the christ is fully arisen within you. It is called Armageddon. Hear you of the term? Armageddon is the battle between the god of your being and your altered-ego, and it is a *powerful* battle! It is not a physical war of weapons. It is a battle that happens within you. It is a battle in which the christ comes forward and is victorious. If your altered-ego sustained, you would certainly die in this battle, but it would be only the death of the *physical* embodiment.

Armageddon is the battle between the god of your being and your altered-ego, and it is a powerful battle!

The second coming of christ is certain upon this plane. Few know it, because most are still entrapped in their dogmas and their little boxes of social consciousness.

Armageddon is the ''divine fire'' of becoming that I have spoken of, and all of you will indeed go through it. It is a battle with *self:* you conquering you, grandly. The christus comes forward and the brain opens up. Then the promise of the utopia of eternal life exists. Now, eternal life is *not* reincarnation; that is repetition. Eternal life is living in the forever now; that is what it means.

All of you have a lot of peeling to do. Now that you know that you and your soulmate can exchange feelings from your souls to gain wisdom, you can use that understanding in your process of peeling so that the christ can come forward.

What I have given you in this audience is not a fearsome teaching. Those who lose their minds over it have picked the words out of context because they have collapsed inwardly. They live in fear; they live in judgment, where they are right and everyone else is wrong. So, of course they will go insane. Well, they *need* to rest, but they will live again.

When you look at the broadness of this teaching, you will understand that you don't have to do anything differently than you are now doing except wholly love what you are and allow your dreams to come to you. Indeed, the natural peeling of an awakening christ will take you from altered-ego into Super-consciousness. In this process, you will find yourselves desiring to do things you never thought of before because your divinity is awakening within you, and it is lifting you from a closed-minded life.

Do you know that two-thirds of your brain is asleep? What do you think it is there for? To plug up the space and give more room for your hair? It is *waiting* to wake up! Consciousness, which is the encapsulation of Is, is the great frontier; it is the adventure. Allowing, loving, and peeling are what permits the dormant mind to wake up. Then you are in Superconsciousness. That is imminent on this plane. That is utopia. It is the meadow, the forest, the lake, the garden of nature. Nature is preparing that place for those who sustain themselves.

When you know everything I've taught you, you'll be a fearless entity. When you know everything I've taught you, you'll own it all and you *will* be happy.

You want to know? Ask yourself. You want to find beauty? Go look in the mirror. You want to live? Watch daybreak.

You want to know? Ask yourself. You want to find beauty? Go look in the mirror. You want to live? Watch daybreak. Simple. So be it.

Audience: So be it.

Ramtha: I have taught you all there is to teach you. You have reached capacity. These teachings are now ready to be lived, to be manifested, to become an adventure. Whatever I say beyond this point is, indeed, repetition. There will come an hour when you will come back to my audience and you will be ready for more—and you will get it, until the hour comes that all of your brain is opened because you love what you are, wholly. Then you are "god-man realized." Then there is no difference between us. Get it? So be it.

Audience: So be it.

Ramtha: I love you grandly. I am the Ram, outrageous entity. I lived once upon your plane and was the biggest bastard of them all. I sought after the Unknown God with vigilance, zeal, and patience. And I am back here to report, *it worked! (Audience cheers and applauds.)* Indeed!

Go and be, be, be, be! Eat, sit, rest, talk, but *be*. Love one another, for whatever you see in them, so you are. And when the hour is two, come back here for a sweet farewell. I have given you all you can take. Indeed! So be it.

Audience: So be it.

Ramtha: You are greatly loved in your *being*. That is all.

Love one another, for whatever you see in them, so you are.

***

Sunday Afternoon Session
January 12, 1986

Ramtha: Indeed! I love you!

Audience: I love you!

Ramtha: There are beauteous and wondrous things that exist on the other side of time. I am one of them. There, one hundred years seem only a moment. And there are moments that seem to be one hundred years in counting.

You have always had a paradoxical view of that which lies beyond time, beyond distance, beyond ongoing space and all of its multifaceted dimensions. You are enamored with the possibilities, but they are also fearful to you. Well, there *are* grand things that lie beyond all measures. There is no demon, no evil, no horrors that go on there. Those are only in your minds; but that is where everything is.

To be here with you I have come from a grand space that is right where you are but which is "beyond beyond." The space I come from is called love. Not even death nor dimensions can separate you from it. It is the great immortal fabric that weaves life.

The space I come from is called love, the great immortal fabric that weaves life.

You have watched and listened and learned from this little body that belongs to one of your own kind. It has been wonderful this way because it has allowed you, with your mind of idealistic form, to look upon me without fear and hear the message. If it had been any other way most of you would not have listened, because you are terrified of that which is beyond the seen.

To come to you this way is a miracle of sorts, a wonderment, to be certain. There is no one like me on this plane of yours, nor will there ever be, for there are few who reach into that which be I. Through this miracle, I have perpetrated upon you a grand display of communication that opens your mind to allow you to have an adventure into a place that is spectacular, and you are going there.

It has been sweet for this wonderment of much conjecture to occur. It is still a wonderment to my daughter's family. But there will come an hour when even they will begin to see and know and own.

I am your angel unseen. I am the wind on high peaks. I am the gentle breeze at midnight. I hear you, because all that you are in the continuum called time is but a moment, and I am the moment.

You will remember me, forever and ever, for what you have learned these days will be with you always. The runners will come to remind you of what, at times, you would like to forget. They won't let you. And the hour will certainly come when you are beyond your outrageous limitations that keep you from exhibiting the miracle called Life, the wonderment called Love, and the brilliance called Mind.

The runners will come to remind you of what, at times, you would like to forget. They won't let you.

Your earth is the emerald of your universe. It hangs in the void like a beautiful gem. It is creation endowed with forever. It is an adventure. It is the home of God. Never desire to run away from it, ever, for it is the adventure that heals the soul. Never take a sunrise for granted. Watch and listen to the quiet, sequential, harmonious movement of life.

When you are beyond all time, distance, and space, beyond the integrities that you have owned, you will own the world and all of its components because you will *be* them.

Winter allows the land to slumber, to regenerate. But what has gone asleep, what is seemingly bare, without fruit or leaf, will return again in spring.

There are those of you in this audience who will pass this plane shortly. You are going into your winter. But the seed of spring, with its fruits and honey blossoms, is in the soul, and you will live again.

There will come an hour when you will reckon with all of the things of life in their natural evolution, and you will own the spirit called Life. Then you are, once again, the king of your dominion. And if, through your obliviousness, you fail to see your beauteous summers and the spice of your autumns, there will be another opportunity, for you will live again. But allow yourselves to enjoy them *now*. Love them *now*. Never regret that you didn't experience enough of life. That only keeps you enslaved in the box of reincarnation. It only makes you spin your wheels.

Never regret that you didn't experience enough of life. That only keeps you enslaved in the box of reincarnation. It only makes you spin your wheels.

Learn to live in silence. Listen to the wind. Feel it! What is it telling you? What are the smells it brings you?

Without this experience here I never would have become who I am. Without the winters upon the land, hard as they were, I never would have desired spring so much. And it was in the spring when I left your plane, for I had lived every moment and every day and every season as they came and went. I *embraced* Life, and I became the Unknown God, which *is* Life itself, the perpetual supporter of all your madness.

I love your plane, greatly. And not one thing shall *ever* come to destroy it. Love it and embrace it also.

How shall you remember me? From the runners? No. When you find the plant which, because it is lonely, wraps around itself to capture the dew and form a pool so that a tiny green frog can live in it—when you find that plant, you will have seen me. When you smell the spice in autumn you will have known my smell. And the next time the moon is waxing across the sky at midnight, open up your curtains and let the light come in. When it lies softly upon you, think about me, for I am the light of the moon.

Many think they know the miracle of what I am. They do not. I am that which is beyond explanation, and be exceedingly glad that I am. Because as long as no one can figure me out, I will be wild and free to make certain that you see where I went. Understand?

I have taught you what you came here to learn, and you got more than you asked for. That is a bargain.

I love you. I have always loved you and always shall. So be it. *(Stands up and walks to the front of the platform. Directly in front of the platform are tables covered with hundreds of glasses of red wine and apple juice.)* You have a choice. There is the ascended grape (I take a fancy to it). And there is the ascended apple (sweet, but it doesn't *quite* do it).

I love you.
I have always loved you
and always shall.

I have bade you drink the water of acidity for cleansing, and you drank it—to everything! The wine represents the ascension of the body, the mind, and the spirit. It is a recognition of God. It is a worthy elixir.

We have prepared the wine. I have looked into its pools and its faces, and there the magic of life exists. I beckon unto the lot of you to come forward in organized lots, two by two, and pick up your glass. After you pick it up, return to your territory and wait until all of your brothers have done the same. Then we will do a *grand* toast to Life. Indeed?

Audience: Indeed!

Ramtha: Now, instruction: The masters who have been bossing you around [staff assisting at the intensive] will come and nag you when it is your time. Get up and do what they ask you to do. And do be courteous and respectful of those receiving their wine, and allow the moment to be one hundred years. So be it.

(After everyone has taken their wine and is seated, Ramtha stands, comes forward, and raises his glass.)

Arise. *(Looking through his wine to the light)* It is liquid rubies! No other planet has liquid rubies. Now you know why I come back.

(Begins the final toast, and the audience repeats.)

Beloved Father,
    that which is the All-in-All,
    the I Am That I Am,
    that which is called Life,
    bring forth unto me
    the completion of I Am.
O beloved mate,

harken unto me this hour,
   that that which be I,
   be That Which Is.
Harken spirit,
   hearken soul:
   Come forth Life.
   I am!
O Father that is,
   O Life forever and ever,
   be I always,
   forever,
   and ever,
   and ever.
To Life!

(Pauses with his glass at his lips, then toasts the audience once more) Go for it! *(Chug-a-lugs his wine)* Ahh! Gusto! *(Audience cheers.)*

There was a lot to be said about being a barbarian. He never needed napkins or cutlery or fine linen or a table. Give him a fire, a spit, a jug of good wine, and whatever is on the hearth, and the entity knew how to live. Well, you are too prim and proper for that.

Go and embrace life. You have many blessings and many runners—the "miracles of knowledge" that I am sending to you. Be happy. For joy is the only thing that the Father, that is ongoing Life, desires for you. Be joyful. Be, allow, and remember. So be it.

Audience: So be it!

Ramtha: I love you. I will see many of you in the desert or in the mountains, and we will have a wondrous hour there. And if you do not find me there, I will be upon the wind. So be it.

***

Appendix

Duvall-Debra

*The Story Of The First Of The Gods
Who Became Man And Woman Upon Terra*

I am Ramtha the Enlightened One, indeed, servant unto that which is termed God Almighty, the beloved Father, the Mother-Father Principle, the Source, the Cause, the Force, the Element, Spirit Divine.

I am Ramtha the Enlightened One, servant unto the Christ, the supreme ruler, the supreme creator, the supreme lawgiver.

I am Ramtha the Enlightened One, servant unto you, my most illustrious brothren. For who *be* you? You are the Father who impregnated himself with thought and became. In becoming, he begat all of you.

You are the Father who impregnated himself with thought and became.

Unto all of you, indeed, who be in such a great fervor to understand who you are, you are the force *of* the Force; you are the light-principle that *created* principle; you are the lawgiver that *became* the law. You are spirit, wisped into reality. In that, you became the sons of the Father, the moving, compulsive element of Thought.

Now, what is it, indeed, that began to create separateness in you? I will help you to understand better.

When the waterous stratum, the aqueous stratum, had beseiged and surrounded the plane of Terra, entering from that which is called the Atrium of the Constants, the element-understanding plane of existence, there came forth, with great excitement, remnants of the warring gods of the plane of Melina. There, in the Atrium of the Constants, they had waited to evolve and lower themselves into the embodiments they had created.

Coming like a great wind, they ble-w-w-w-w-w-w their fervor over all the lands and the oceans. And the great tree looked up and began to bend and bow before the beauty of its creator.

The "wind" split itself and became a northern and a southern and an eastern and a western for the purpose of carrying its whispers of energy throughout this plane to places where groups of gods, in their "colonized selves" or "Lord Houses," could commune with each other for the advancement of the human spirit.

All of the gods came at once save one group.

All of the gods came at once save one group. The one group that remained in the Atrium of the Constants would later follow as the future children of their forerunners.

Immediately as the gods came upon this plane to their chosen areas, behold: As they began to manifest themselves by lowering and splitting their splendid selves, they became brilliant lights upon the land, brighter than your noonday sun. (There is noted in your summaries of ancient history, religions that worshipped the coming of a brilliant peoples. It was they themselves! In future lives they would worship and write their own history.)

As the gods began, through contemplation, to lower their vibrations from splendid thought-light, they all became shadowy into mass; and, in the final understanding they became mass . . . heavy, heavy, heavy upon this plane of a three-dimensional understanding.

Upon whatever continental plane (or country, as you term it) they took form into the heaviness of the bodily movement, they immediately began to attune themselves to what is called the environmental home of their own creation. Thus there became, simultaneously, the five great "races" as you term them, differing according to skin color to permit them to live and survive upon that which they had created.

In a land upon Terra, there began the first life of a man and a woman, the first existence of one god who lowered all its creative self and split itself into the two so that it could experience the adventure of mankind. I will give you a name. The name did exist and still exists, even unto this hour. (The entities of whom I will speak are but two of a multi-faceted mass of entities who came upon the plane at this time.) One entity's name was Duvall-Debra Badu. The two names specify the unit of one, while "Badu" means "God essence of."

Duvall-Debra was male in his gender, being that which is called, in your scientific understanding, a positive electrical charge. Of his body, he had that which is called the erection staff and the permissiveness of the seed that lay within his loin sac.

Created *by the same god* was Debra-Duvall, who was what is called a "*womb*-man," meaning: man being with womb, or "woman" as you term it. The womb did not have the seed; instead it had that which is called the egg, which would be punctured by the seed, the treasure within a man's loins.

Debra-Duvall was, and still is, the explicit soulmate of the entity called Duvall-Debra. She was what is called, in your scientific understanding, a negative electrical charge. Of her creation, she was not *less than* Duvall-Debra but was the *perfected* extension of him to permit the exercise of copulation for the advancement of the human species. For a god can "seed" an embodiment for another god to enter this plane only when it divides itself to become both positive and negative electrical charges.

Debra-Duvall was, and still is, the explicit soulmate of Duvall-Debra.

The knowledge of their heritage was not readily accessible to Duvall-Debra and Debra-Duvall; for when the god who had become the two lowered its light, its thought processes became heavier, thus more difficult. But still, in their first advancement upon Terra, their first life upon your plane, both Debra and Duvall were ever so powerful in their nurturing of pure thought.

Duvall looked upon Debra's eyes and saw them as being explicit in their beauty. Duvall did not *know* the spectacularness of his own eyes until he looked upon Debra's, for she had *same* of her eye. And let me tell you of the color of his eyes.

RAMTHA INTENSIVE: SOULMATES

The round perimeters were brilliant snowy white, and from there they went into a dark blue luster that merged with a yellow luster, giving the illusion of a sea. From there they went into a brighter hue of hazel, into the condensation of the perfect lens, or what is called the black of the eye. The eyes were wondrous, *wondrous* creations from Thought, for they had the ability to assess matter, or Thought in its slowest frequency.

Duvall looked at Debra and was in awe of her, for he could not imagine another creation that could have been lovelier. Duvall looked into the eyes of Debra and saw that they were ever-changing, the blue at times seeping into the brilliant snowy white. And he loved the wondrous eyes of Debra (yet he did not know and understand the action of love).

And he loved the wondrous eyes of Debra, yet he did not know and understand the action of love.

As Duvall looked upon the color of Debra's completed flesh, it brought to mind the radiance of light and its expanding hues. (The color spectrum on Terra was not that of elevated thought, only of completed thought, the ending of thought in matter. But in that, it had the advantage of being the only level of Thought that had colors that were heaviest in color-light vibration.) Such a wonderful hue of rose blushed high upon her forehead, cheeks, and lips, which were dewy and mellow.

Duvall touched the firm brows of Debra and found them to be moist. As he touched the thick and wondrous lashes that framed her beautiful eyes, he saw that her chin was cleft and her throat was like a column of marble. His touch gently moved to her shoulder, which was delicate yet boldly defined, and along her arm, which was graceful. He saw that her arm extended from her shoulder without a break in its movement, for it was part of her shoulder. Moving his hand down her arm and unto her wrist, he saw her hand move! And he looked upon her fingers, with their delicate creases, and saw on the hardened part of her finger tips, the same blush that was high upon her cheeks, and he found them lovely. Lovely!

Duvall stood back and gazed at Debra's body. With outstretched arms he gently touched her breasts and found them to be warm and supple, erect and firm, with only the slightest whisper of blush upon the furthermost point of their beauty. Under her breasts he found a beautiful waist structure, with skin draped so lightly upon it that it captivated the eye.

Duvall marvelled at the creation of something so lovely, so soft, so wonderful in its color. Gently he moved his hand down her smooth and flawless thighs until he found a bend in her leg. At the bend he found a small dimple. On the other side, Duvall found that the hardest point of this beloved creature's leg was her knee. He moved his hand down her leg to her delicately formed and rounded calf and on to the slender mass of her ankle, where he found a hardness. Holding her small foot in his hand, Duvall moved it up . . . and down. He looked at the graceful bones of her foot and saw that the tips of her toes were of the same blush as her cheeks.

When Debra gazed upon that which was looking upon her in amazement, she saw that the color of Duvall's hair was like autumn, and she thought it was wonderful! And when she peered upon his hair to find it autumn in color, she found that her own hair was the same wondrous color.

As Debra began to look at Duvall, she saw the same loveliness of the eyes that Duvall had beheld. And she saw a firm nostril that was elongated and large, that permitted a massiveness of air to enter therein. And she saw them flair! She looked upon his lips, which were firm and expressive and large, and she saw that they completed themselves upon a jawline that was curved and broad. And she saw a neck that was stout, and shoulders that were broad, and arms that were thick and heavy and beautiful.

Upon Duvall's arms, Debra beheld the same color of autumn that was upon his head, curled neatly in rows of patterned perfection. She saw a hand that was broad and long and lovely, with a hardness encrusted upon the tips of his fingers, as if some remarkable thing had touched it as a final act to its creativity.

Debra stood back to see that Duvall's chest was broad, and that it heaved as he breathed through flaired nostrils. Upon his chest, where the heart lies, she saw nipples that were smaller

Under her breasts he found a beautiful waist structure, with skin draped so lightly upon it that it captivated the eye.

than hers, that were flattened yet lovely and beautiful. And she saw that Duvall's waist was nigh the same as his hips, which were smaller than hers. And where the legs of Duvall split, she saw a wonderful creation wherein lay his treasure and the hope of generations to come. And his legs, they were muscular, with knees that were broad and firm, and calves that were stout, and feet that were long and broad to permit the stance of the greatness of the entity called Duvall.

As Duvall and Debra gazed at one another, what they saw was the reflection of the other. Each in its own beautiful way had been formulated, from god to man, in the greatest design possible to permit the interchange of man and woman upon a plane which, long in the making, was now prepared. Thus, each had the perfection of its embodiment which would create, of itself, the perfect seed for a lineage to come.

Each had the perfection of its embodiment which would create, the perfect seed for a lineage to come.

Now, where was love? One never possesses any one thing until he has first contemplated it, for the possession can never be experienced and reveled in until it is first realized in contemplative thought. Thus, once the touch was felt and certain, and the two had contemplated the loveliness and beauty of one another, then the fire of the loin and of the womb began. And when each made the thought go forth into the other, there came forth the first fertile act of Duvall-Debra and Debra-Duvall. Through the wondrous creations that their own perfect one-self had now become, did they permit themselves to come together and cling together, and to bring forth the seed from the loin and erected staff of Duvall into the wonderful egg of Debra, the nest of histories to come.

Upon committal of his seed into an outward projection, Duvall looked into the eyes of Debra and saw himself, and he loved his image. And Debra looked into the eyes of Duvall and loved her image. When the seed came forth and found the egg, there became the perfect image that they had seen in one another. At that moment, behold: From the Atrium of the Constants there came forth another god, one who had been awaiting its turn to lower itself into the embodiments of a man and a woman upon the plane of Terra.

When the staff of Duvall was limp with its weariness, he laid beside his beautiful woman, and his beautiful woman laid beside him. And Duvall, in loving himself grandly, loved all that he saw in Debra, and Debra the same in he. Love was now understood. Thus the union had begun of the two who would forever belong unto one another. Their light force had evolved itself into the pleasure of created force, called matter, to begin a new adventure into Life.

When the staff of Duvall was limp with its weariness, he laid beside his beautiful woman.

Life upon Terra truly began through a marketplace of ideals coming forth and being exchanged between one another. As thought became industrious, industry soon became apparent in the working orders of the land. Soon, what is called the science of light propellants began a great industry, and light was used regularly upon this plane for intermittant travel and the transmuting of things. As values of exchange became apparent between all of the gods, Duvall began the processes of creation through the marketplace of ideals.

Into his first life upon Terra, there came forth an entity from the blessed womb and the nest of Debra-Duvall. The entity, called Arius, was the positive electrical charge of one great god who had lowered itself from the Atrium of the Constants and split its light force. Through copulation, an act of creation of the first plane, this god was thus permitted to become into embodiments created by other gods, the grandest thing that one god was to give to his brothers through the action of love.

Arius was the happiness of Debra and Duvall. He came forth into their lives and was nursed by Debra and held closely to her soul. Always love was there. Duvall, stately and wondrous, was pleased to have the comradship of another brother, another god, in the terms called peace.

Now, the competitive spirit of the gods divine lived verily amongst all who were upon Terra. Thus, once commerce in the marketplace had begun from the exchange of ideas in mass, soon to rise up again was one god trying to outdo the other. It was during this process and this time that Duvall began a comradship with other gods who would rally with one another in acts of commerce.

There soon came unto Duvall's understanding the desire for more knowledge in order to equate his thought into a more productive form, for already others were doing it quite well. In the process of desiring to become more, Duvall spent long periods of time away from Debra, for he was caught up in the competition of his beloved brothers in the ongoing marketplace. Thus, through his attitude, an attitude which had been pure in its conception, Duvall separated himself from the tender love of Debra, his beloved equal, who was busy at her task of bringing forth and recognizing and sharing with her beloved Arius, a most remarkable god. Debra, with outstretched arms, would often call out to Duvall, the mirror of her being, to let her love and touch and hold and be a part of the "firstness of her first." But Duvall, being caught up in creative thoughts, did not heed the pleas of his beloved Debra.

Duvall, being caught up in creative thoughts, did not heed the pleas of his beloved Debra.

Soon, Duvall assimilated himself as being an authority of sorts in "giving and taking." Thus there became an attitude of superiority from him. When this attitude became apparent in Duvall, it soon became apparent with all of his comrades. And when all became of the attitude that their status was somewhat different, there became a separateness between them, a grave error indeed.

One day, upon the experimentation with a force of light, Duvall, putting forth light into a reflector to align it in a particular direction, aligned his mirror at a most improper angle. When the light projectile was given off and reflected, it was in Duvall's path, and he became pierced by a light swifter and greater than any sword or explosion that you know of. At that moment, Duvall's body became of death. His body, which had been brought into being at his own hands, now, at his own hands, had perished, for it was severed greatly.

Duvall suffered his first death on Terra. Though his body had perished, death had not daunted the spirit and soul of his being that gave credence to his liquid eyes and wonderful presence.

Duvall was now caught up in a void liken unto a wind vacuum. From there he could see the Atrium of the Constants, where his beloved brothers were watching him. As he looked to assess where he had come from, he saw his body, and he saw Debra and his son, Arius. He called out for Debra, and he called out for Arius, whose laughter would drown out the wind . . . but they could not hear him.

Duvall tried again and again, but still they could not hear. Then he saw his friends, and he tried to become unto them, but he could not. As Duvall watched them look upon his body, he saw that they had not sorrow or pity upon their faces but rather an assessing attitude.

Debra, who loved the being of her being, or husbandman as he is called, learned of her tears and learned of sorrow. And she called out for Duvall, "Being of my being, blue of my blue, body of my body, where be you, Duvall?" And Debra, now recognizing death in the body, a most shocking element, wept over the body of her precious Duvall.

Debra, now recognizing death in the body, a most shocking element, wept over the body of her precious Duvall.

Duvall, who could neither speak to his beloved nor cry for the help of his gathering friends, was most perplexed. He was now in the void, created by the attitude of superiority. From there he could not ascend back into the Brotherhood, for he had experienced "superiority," a mode of thinking in which he would now, unfortunately, refer to his own beloved self in lesser terms.

There came unto Duvall, through contemplative thought, a realization of how to become out of his predicament. So he spoke forth a plea unto the Atrium of the Constants, and he asked his beloved brothers there for the void and the separateness to be no longer. And he called out to them, "Please do not come into the light of Arius so that you may come unto this plane. Do permit me to become again through this son of mine so that I may make things better with all whom I have separated from me."

Being of good hearts, the gods agreed. Upon agreeance, their will to become the child of Arius was released, and the light of Duvall came into the spectacular light field of his beloved son so he might be born again.

*Arius found for himself
the perfect receptor,
the perfect beauty
that he, Arius, loved
above all other things:
himself in another.*

Arius had come into manhood and was learning of the movement of the loin. Seeking a mirror for the beauty of his being, he found an enchantress, an entity who was like the moon in her loveliness, for little by little she would show him more of her beauty.

Arius became caught up with the enchantress, and soon he could not bear to be without her any longer. So Arius (with the urging of his beloved father) found for himself the perfect receptor, the perfect beauty that he, Arius, loved above all other things—himself in another.

Arius proclaimed that the enchantress was, above all things, his greatest desire as completed creation. When they came together, like Duvall and Debra had done, they discovered one another's beauty and being, and they expressed it. And the thought of love became a fertile being, conceived of the infinite form, that would permit Duvall to become again upon the plane of Terra.

Duvall had never been a child. Thus he took great delight in becoming a part of *another's* created form. To understand the meaning of sharing, to understand the meaning of procreation, to make things anew, Duvall became the child. Thus, through the womb of the enchantress came forth Duvall in a wondrous body for the purpose of no longer seeing himself as different from those whom he loved but a part of them. (In your understanding, Duvall would now have Debra as the grandmother of his being.)

As a little boy, Duvall loved his grandmother, loved his mother, the enchantress, and loved Arius as a wonderful "son-father." And he saw them all in an evenness. He was respectful of his grandmother (who did not know that he be Duvall), and he gave unto her kindness and joy and a jubilant heart. He would always listen to her wisdom concerning creation and things of the marketplace, and he learned readily from her.

After his grandmother was no more of this plane, Duvall grew forth into his life and became an industrious entity who saw fairness and evenness in all exchanges. He was, in part, what is called "balanced." Noted for his balance of attitude he grew long into his years. He had not taken another to his bed, or taken another to look deep into his eyes so that he may see himself, for his concern had been for "balance."

One day, as Duvall was returning from the marketplace where all went to assess the ideals of perfection and to exchange greater ideas, he came upon a lovely entity, a small girl of the age of fourteen in years. The entity was going to the marketplace to assess the thought of the upcoming marriage of her being to someone who would be perfect for her being. When Duvall stopped to look into her eyes, he saw in her eyes, his. The young woman, who no longer had hair the color of autumn but that of the sun, gazed back upon the eyes of Duvall and saw herself. Behold! Duvall's beloved Debra had come once again, and yet he knew not whence she had come. They had found one another through that which is termed the "thought processes" of Debra.

When Duvall stopped to look into her eyes, he saw in her eyes, his.

Like they had done once before, Duvall and Debra came together and brought forth, through the splendor of copulation and love, a daughter, a wondrous creature of light and beauty. And Duvall was caught up with her, the mirror of his love for Debra. And she was *wondrous*—beyond the enchantress, beyond Debra, for she was the creation of the height of perfected love that had sought to express itself anew.

As a little girl, the entity had silken hair that was darker than the palette of midnight, with curls that were wild and moving and free. And when she brought up her wondrous head, her hair would fall gracefully upon her shoulders. The eyes of this entity were of the hue of seas that you have not seen in this time. So blue were they that they were wondrous to peer at. They were so wondrous that when one was caught up with them he saw little else. The little girl was, unto her father's eye, perfect. Duvall, who rallied himself in the perfection of his sweet daughter, loved her greatly, like he loved Debra. And he took great pleasure in watching the continual growth of the splendid creature.

y the time Duvall's daughter had reached the age of four-
n in years, she was already an exquisite woman, for her
ason of womanhood had already come to bear. Her breasts
d ripened, her cheeks were at a flush, and her eyes were
lled with wonder and adventure. Duvall knew that it was the
time for his beloved daughter to assess herself in thought for
the husbandman of her being. And yet, when he came,
Duvall, who had never before experienced the passion of jealousy, did so; and he became protective of his daughter, wish-
ing not for her to marry. His daughter laughed at her beloved
father, for she knew him to be a man of passion who was bent
on finding a man of such passion for her, which she had.

Duvall forbade the man to take his beloved daughter from
his house. If they were to marry, they must live there with
Duvall and Debra. But this splendid man, this god, who loved
Duvall's beautiful daughter, had already prepared a kingdom
for her, and thus refused the "kind" offer.

Duvall, in his haste, threatened the man, grabbed his
daughter by her tender arm, and pulled her back. The daughter, looking up into her father's eyes, had experienced a new
attitude in her father, and she was greatly perplexed by it. She
gently took her father's hand from her sweet arm and said unto
him, "Father, this is my desire. This is to whom I belong.
This is my life." With that, the young woman turned unto her
beloved man, and they both left the audience of Duvall.

Duvall was grieved in his heart, for would he ever again see
the splendor of Debra in his beautiful daughter? And he de-
spised the one who had taken his gem from his life. Debra,
wonderful Debra, who understood her husbandman's passion
but not his anger, beseeched him to calm himself. But Duvall
wept, and he wept, and he wept.

This wondrous story is a truthful one. The entities I have
spoken of all existed. This story is a story of the creation of
man's attitudes through perfect love and how he has limited
them.

When Duvall came back again as the son of Arius and the

enchantress, he did indeed perfect his "supremacy" attitude towards others. But in his pursuit of life, he erroneously became of the attitudes of jealousy and possessiveness over his beautiful daughter, forgetting the independence of the godship that she was.

When Duvall perished late in age in that life, he did so with gloom, and he did weep, for he had to come yet again. And he had to wait a long time after all whom he loved had passed this plane, even his beloved daughter, who perished through acts of her thought processes. And his story has gone on, and on, and on, even unto this hour.

His story has gone on, and on, and on, even unto this hour.

Has Duvall reckoned with his attitudes of limitation? He has tried, earnestly. Yet he has permitted himself the extravagance of becoming involved in petty illusions and limited desires. Thus he hath experienced deaths in the number of ten thousand and thirty upon this plane.

That which is call jealousy, hate, envy, war, despise and judgment—they can be summed up as all of the limited attitudes of man. And what has given all of them credence has been what is called "love." But as long as man continues to justify his pettiness of attitude in the name of love, he will have to die ten thousand and thirty deaths at the hands of them to perchance attain a level of "complete love godship," so that he may go back unto the Atrium and pass beyond it into Thought.

Your children are *not* created from your loins and your wombs. You provide, through the exchange of love—or lust—the opportunity for a great god to come forth to complete whatever it needs in order to perfect itself and become a light unto the world. But you do not have *ownership* of its spirit. You never will. And to lose your children? You have been together *eons* in your time, one life right after another. Duvall would never lose his daughter. She would be, in his lives to come, his mother, his sister, his grandmother, his grandfather, his enemy, his ruler, his servant, and his friend.

You never lose anything. If you love in freedom you gain *everything,* including the opportunity to distinguish yourself from God into you—you who are learning the illusions of limited thought—back into God in all its beauty.

You are always God! That *is* a truth. You are always the Source. Yet you continuously disrupt your lives through pettiness in your beings; thus you will continuously evolve yourself, life after life, into trying to become better. Never *try* to become better—know that you *are* better! There is a difference in that statement, I assure you.

Do permit yourself the patience to contemplate your judgments, to contemplate your decisions, to assess your attitude in regard to anyone else. And determine for yourself if the obsession in the moment is worth ten thousand more lifetimes. If it is, enjoy eternity.

I am Ramtha the Enlightened One, exquisite teacher, learned entity, and lover of all of your beings. Ponder what I have given unto you this eloquent moment, and learn from it. Be at peace and of warm heart and good cheer. 'Tis the season of your rebirth. Be exceedingly glad for that. So be it.

***